Becoming a
Modern
Contemplative

Becoming a
Modern
Contemplative

A Psychospiritual Model for Personal Growth

Richard B. Patterson

A Campion Book

Loyola University Press
Chicago

Loyola University Press
3441 North Ashland Avenue
Chicago, Illinois 60657

Library of Congress Cataloging-in-Publication

The poem "Black Lung Marriage" by Richard B. Patterson
originally appeared in *Appalachian Heritage* 18, 1 (winter
1990): 63, and is used by permission.

Cover and interior design by Nancy Gruenke.
Cover direction by Frederick Falkenberg
and Jill Mark Salyards.
Electronic artwork by Tammi Longsjo.

Patterson, Richard B.
Becoming a modern contemplative: a psychospiritual model
for spiritual growth/Richard B. Patterson.
   p.   cm.
   Includes bibliographical references and index.
   ISBN 0-8294-0814-2
   1. Contemplation. 2. Meditation. 3. Spiritual life.
BV5091.C7P38 1995
248.3'4'019—dc20   94-37758
                              CIP
                              Rev.

For my brother,

Robert A. Patterson, Jr.,

with gratitude

Contents

Acknowledgments

I have been blessed with many teachers, as I have stumbled along the path described in this book. With a grateful heart, I am happy to thank them.

Dr. Richard Park gave me a timely word of encouragement on the section on journaling and helped me develop the image of the clown, an image that would eventually tie the other four images together. He also invited me to present a workshop with him, from which emerged the section on writing poetry. Gail Edwards selflessly read the manuscript and offered detailed feedback and much-valued affirmation. Beyond that, she is a trusted companion on journeys shared.

Dr. Gerald Bryan has been my valued traveling partner for many years. Humble man that he is, he influences me in large and small ways, yet never takes credit for his very real presence in my life. Most especially, he has taught me the way of friendship.

Father Joseph Downey of Loyola University Press has approached my work with affirmation and commitment. His belief in the value of my words remains a source of great appreciation for me. June Sawyers, also of Loyola University Press, took on the task of polishing my prose and did so with thoroughness and sensitivity. I am genuinely grateful for her patience and guidance.

My wife, Pinzy, has shared with me the gift of long-term marriage. Her creativity has inspired me, and her encouragement always makes a difference. Whatever I know of loving, committed relationships I have learned from and with her.

My children Matt, Becky, Ben, and Andy have graced me with many blessings. They have helped me to play, to wonder, to listen. With each of them, I have shared special moments of the mystical side of life.

Many persons have shared their stories with me over the years during the course of consultations. The abundant lessons they have provided will continue to guide me.

Introduction

When most of us hear the term *contemplative,* we think of monks in remote monasteries, of shadowed hoods and Gregorian chants. Perhaps we think of the peace and of the quiet of such settings with a certain longing.

For some, however, the theme of contemplation has touched their lives beyond monastery walls. Many people have been greatly influenced by contemplative writers such as Thomas Merton and Abraham Heschel or contemplatives in action such as Susan B. Anthony and Henri Nouwen. Others flock to the countryside to contemplate nature or sit in silent awe, listening to a particular piece of music. Still others touch the contemplative life by watching in amazement a film clip of baseball player Willie Mays chasing and, at the last conceivable moment, catching a 400-foot drive by Vic Wertz of the Cleveland Indians.

The image of the contemplative life appealed to me at a very early age. In *The Hero Journey in Dreams,* Jean and Wallace Clift (1988) invite readers to recall favorite childhood stories. I did not have to think long. I remembered the joy of my own favorite tale, *The Story of Ferdinand the Bull* (Leaf 1946).

For those of you unfamiliar with the story, I'll give a quick summary. The tale begins with these lyrical words "Once upon a time in Spain, there was a little bull and his name was Ferdinand." While the other young bulls dreamed of bullfights in Madrid, Ferdinand preferred to sit under a tree and "smell the flowers." When Ferdinand was grown, promoters came from Madrid to select bulls for bullfight competitions. Disinterested, Ferdinand wandered off to sit under his favorite cork tree. Unfortunately, rather than enjoying his peaceful day, he sat inadvertently on a bumblebee. The pain from the sting sent Ferdinand roaring and snorting all over the pasture, greatly impressing the men from Madrid. For this reason, Ferdinand was chosen. Once he was in the ring, however, his gentle nature returned. Rather than play the role of the ferocious bull, he sat down in the middle of the ring to smell the flowers that decorated the hair of many of the ladies in attendance. A complete failure, he was returned to pasture. "And for all I know he is sitting there still, under his favorite cork tree, smelling the flowers just quietly. He is very happy" (Ibid.).

Recently, my daughter, Becky, became a bit flustered over exams and music competitions. I talked to my brother and discussed Becky's situation with him. "Why don't you have her read *Ferdinand the Bull?*" he suggested. My daughter's struggle and my brother's "solution" inspired me to write this book.

Contemplative psychology is a subject that you are not likely to find in many psychology book indices. In part this is because the subject matter is actually quite broad. Second, the assumed passivity of the contemplative does not hold great appeal for psychologists and other professional helpers who much prefer to see results. Further, contemplative psychology stands at the crossroads of psychology and spirituality, a street corner that helping professionals are still reluctant to acknowledge.

We will explore a variety of human experiences and states within the scope of contemplative psychology. These subjects range from mysticism to social justice, from baseball to bigotry. My goal is to encourage everyone to become a modern contemplative. I will argue that one can be a contemplative in traffic, at one's desk, while eating a meal, or attending (or teaching) a class. For, above all, contemplation involves movement *into* life, not *away* from it!

First some clarity regarding terminology is necessary. The scope of contemplative psychology and the activities and attitudes of a modern contemplative are not confined to contemplation. Attitudes and activities include meditation, spontaneous experiences of wonder, journaling, the psychology of solitude, and the role of social justice. The activity of contemplation itself can mean different things to different people. By contemplation, some writers refer to a specific prayer form that involves an emptying of one's ego through fairly repetitive meditations, such as the Jesus prayer or by simply counting as one breathes. For others, contemplation means simply to be "with"—without any need to be productive or to solve problems. My own preference is to view contemplation as the simple act of beholding. It is more than mere watching since it includes the emotional response of wonder as well as the possibility of an altered state of consciousness. To behold implies a nonverbal sense of connectedness. Meditation involves a more dynamic interaction with the object of meditation, particularly in terms of active thought processes and verbal activity. In meditation, I am "talking with" the object of my meditation; in contemplation I am simply "being with." Meditation, however, is often the doorway to contemplation.

To become a modern contemplative, one must understand certain stances much like a student of the martial arts needs to master particular techniques in order to fully appreciate the discipline. Five stances, in particular, guide the growth and development of the modern contemplative: simplicity, self-discipline, sensuality, detachment, and gratitude. These stances will be examined in chapter 1.

The journey of the modern contemplative will be examined in chapters 2, 3, 4, and 5. Certain necessities are required to make this journey. They include a journal, solitude, a "sacred place," and a companion.

Chapter 6 examines four images—the meditator, the contemplative, the mystic, and the prophet—that capture the essence of being a modern contemplative, images that describe a type of movement rather than static states or stages. These four icons underlie the spiritual and psychological dimension of the movement. A fifth image, that of the clown, is offered somewhat whimsically as a symbol that has the potential to unify the four movements of the modern contemplative.

Finally, chapter 7 identifies messengers who can direct the modern contemplative to aspects of life that are rich sources of contemplation and that can provide the modern contemplative with the proper messages to bring back to society in a prophetic manner. The image of the trailhead is also introduced. Given that a trailhead is a hiker's starting point, it is an appropriate symbol for the modern contemplative.

In the back matter the reader will find an annotated bibliography and a complete reference list to works cited in the text.

Who should aspire to become a modern contemplative? While the role of the modern contemplative is open to all, a few special groups may wish to seriously consider it. These groups include:

1. Individuals who manifest symptoms of severe stress. Such individuals would include those with stress-based health problems, those in high-stress work settings, or those with other stress-related problems such as sleep disturbance, irritability, or self-destructive behavior (overeating).
2. Individuals who have "lost" their way. Such individuals would include anyone struggling at mid-life, anyone considering a major career change, anyone grappling with a crisis of faith or religion, or anyone troubled by addiction to mind-altering drugs (including alcohol).
3. Helping professionals and paraprofessionals; this path is recommended for anyone entrusted with the care of mind, body, and soul.

Other groups of people naturally aspire to the contemplative life. Prominent among them are children and the elderly. These persons might be looked upon as valued teachers.

Finally, a few myths about everyday contemplatives need to be dispelled:

1. *Contemplatives always feel calm and are at peace.* On the contrary, as the contemplative acquires a heightened sense of connection, the individual may experience outrage at injustice, sadness over loss, and so forth. To be connected involves sharing pain.
2. *Contemplatives are detached from the world.* What appears to be detachment from the world is actually a healthy resolution of the contemplative's need for control.
3. *Contemplatives live in poverty.* The guiding economic theme for the contemplative is simplicity, not poverty. Poverty is viewed by the contemplative as a manifestation of injustice.
4. *Meditation and contemplation are mental activities.* Becoming a modern contemplative involves the embracing of a lifestyle, which includes regular mental activities. But to *become* a modern contemplative involves changes in behavior and a greater openness to emotions.

To some, the contemplative life may seem frivolous, a luxury. Why, then, should one even consider pursuing this goal? There are several reasons. The world needs peacemakers, and they can develop only by making peace within themselves. We cannot love our worldly enemy and still hate the enemy within. Second, we need to recover the capacity for wonder. Through wondrous contemplation, we will again appreciate nature, not destroy or manipulate it. Finally, many of us have lost our way, no longer able to find anything meaningful to guide or help us. Increasingly, we turn to drugs, to alcohol, to food, to sex for solace. The answers are still within and among us. We just need to listen.

Certain aspects of the contemplative life go against our grain. Contemplatives are nonintrusive, not intent on changing persons, places, or things. They prefer to approach life with mutual respect and appreciation. Consequently, to outsiders the contemplative appears to be unproductive or passive. The contemplative does not see persons in terms of their differences, such as rich versus poor or young versus old or male versus female. Thus, a modern contemplative who sees women as no different than men in terms of "priestly" qualities might not be welcome in some churches that think otherwise. Further, the contemplative is nonviolent. In pursuing the contemplative life, one runs the risk of being labeled "radical" or, perhaps, just plain "weird."

Part of the contemplative path involves a journey inward, whereby an individual contemplates one's inner self. Sometimes what we find and observe within ourselves is less than flattering. These revelations can even be frightening. The modern contemplative does not avoid such self-discoveries but sees them as an integral facet of an inner reality. As contemplatives, we cannot selectively choose our inner or outer world.

As with so much in the spiritual domain, the contemplative life cannot be achieved directly. Rather it becomes real as one possesses other attributes or pursues other stances. Individuals do not practice contemplation as such; they become a contemplative as they practice the stance of simplicity.

The call to the contemplative path is a call to a simple, gentle life—not removed from life, but guided by a deep and abiding respect. It is a type of simplicity and respectfulness once prevalent among Native Americans. Is it too late for us to learn from them? Perhaps not. The various tribes of the Algonquian nation, who once roamed the forests of my home state of Pennsylvania, still have much to teach us through their stories and legends. After reading *The Last Algonquian* by Theodore L. Kazimiroff (1982) I was moved to write the following poem:

Algonquian Requiem

How I long to pass through life
Like an Algonquian in the woods.
I'd leave things undisturbed
Having taken with respect
Only what I'd need
And nothing more.

My campfire would be small
But always to be shared,
A place where stories can be told
And not forgotten.
The point (if there must be a point)
Would be

That I can tell your story
And you mine
At other travelers' fires
In winter
But with no sign of us
Come morning.

And when my time comes
To select my own star
I'll be content
If the scent
Of sweat and Old Spice
Lingers as my legacy.

1

The Stances

1

To approach life as a contemplative requires practicing a variety of transforming stances, some of which you may have already incorporated into your own particular path.

Simplicity

In discussing the theme of liberation theology, Matthew Fox noted that so-called First World nations were largely uninterested in hearing about the plight of Third World countries and their imprisonment by poverty. He forcefully challenges the notion that we of the First World are free of shackles, describing First World poverty as ". . . spiritual impoverishment that is palpable where consumerism reigns and materialism runs people's lives" (1991, 78). The primary symptoms of our own impoverishment are our addictions, our apathy, our boredom.

We are driven by a quest for "stuff" and, sadly, find our opinion of ourselves trapped within the prison walls of wealth and achievement. Such drive is a major roadblock on the path of the modern contemplative. One can counterbalance these selfish urges by practicing the stance of simplicity, a stance dramatically described by Richard Foster as ". . . the glad trumpet call of liberation to all who are oppressed by reputation, wealth, and power" (1981, 42).

When we hear the word simplicity many of us think of the Amish or perhaps of the ascetic life of Saint Francis of Assisi and immediately reject the notion, either because we treasure our modern conveniences or (more often, I believe) because we despair that simplicity is a possibility in our lives. In fact simplicity is well within our reach. We simply need to substitute quality for quantity, substance for appearance.

A great paradox has emerged involving the Shaker interpretation of simplicity. Shaker furniture was crafted in a way that manifested simple beauty, so well, in fact, that the pieces are now avidly sought by wealthy antique collectors. Sadly, the spiritual vision of the Shaker crafters has been lost. I recall watching a television program about the Shakers in which one Shaker woman spoke about the frequency of rain on the days when a local auction of Shaker furniture was held. Some thought of the rain as "the old Shakers crying."

How often do I do something "well" as opposed to "quickly"? How often have I calculated the number of hours of therapy necessary to achieve a certain level of income? At times, I have listened well or counseled well; other times I have not been so attentive.

Simplicity is never an achieved commodity. Rather we allow the stance of simplicity to stand in contrast to our sense of drivenness, thereby creating a sort of constant tension and need for balancing.

Foster describes succinctly the theme of substance when he says: "Stop trying to impress people with your clothes and impress them with your life" (Ibid., 73). I would only add that the less we try to impress people with our lives, the more impressive we become.

Similarly, sportswriter Thomas Boswell places this qualitative dimension of simplicity squarely between success and excellence: "Success can burn up the person who achieves it. Excellence usually feeds whoever has it" (1990, *xvii*). If simplicity contains the pursuit of excellence, rather than success, then, according to Boswell, simplicity is what we find "at the heart of the order."

Think for a moment of some persons you may have known who personified the simple life. In her later years my Aunt Dorothy lived in a small apartment in California. She had a small television set, mainly for watching the news. She ate simple meals. She had no car but walked or used public transportation to get around. She did have one "luxury," however— a radio and cassette player so that she could enjoy her great love: music. Dorothy was a rather unremarkable person who quietly passed through life, seemingly leaving little behind. And yet I remember her vividly. I inherited her love of music and have passed it on to my children, especially to my daughter. I also have shared with friends and loved ones a few stories of her simple acts of kindness and generosity. I am a better person having walked with her awhile. Others have touched my life with their simplicity. I have turned to them as teachers.

What does living a life of simplicity mean at a practical level? To assume the stance of simplicity, must we stand naked in the marketplace like Saint Francis?[1] Such an assumption typically throws people off. First, we must assess the level at which we battle distraction throughout our day. Am I always thinking hours or days ahead? How much do I worry about the future? How well do I complete my daily activities, both the important and the unimportant ones?

Second, we need to assess our attitudes about "stuff." We can do this several ways. How old is the car you drive? How long do you keep the cars that you buy? How many appliances do you have (including entertainment appliances)? How well do you function when those appliances are in the shop? Who cleans your house? your clothes? What are your priorities when it comes to spending money? How much do you spend on clothes? How often do you buy something because you "want" it, not because you need it?

A central feature of simplicity is to focus on sufficiency. Usually when I pray for money or material needs I do not win the jackpot, but I do receive a sufficiency. For me this has been an important lesson—to learn to accept with joy and gratitude that which is sufficient. When I attend to what is sufficient, I then discover that I have more to share, a realization, I may add, that is at the heart of the loaves and fishes story. Through his teaching, Jesus was able to make the crowd realize what they already had was enough. Thus, when it came time to eat, the people produced bread and fish, which they had been hoarding "just in case." When all necessary needs were met, an abundance remained.

For this reason, I need to honestly assess my attitudes about the poor and to confront any areas that may suggest bigotry or prejudice. How often do I dismiss the poor as lazy? What are my attitudes about the welfare system in the United States? about Medicare and Medicaid? How do I react to news of government cuts in social programs? How closely do I follow the struggles and conflicts in Central America, South America,

Africa, and other Third World regions? And for those in the helping professions, how willing are we to extend special considerations to the poor, the elderly, and the homeless so that they may receive our services?

These are only some of the issues we need to address if we wish to seriously pursue a life of simplicity. When you find yourself motivated by material gain, you need to learn how to "make do" and, if possible, communicate with those individuals from whom you feel different. Listen to yourself. Try to determine if those obstacles are based on fundamental differences or material possessions. You may need to open yourself to your own inner poverty.

Richard Rohr discusses four forms of poverty in his book *Simplicity: The Art of Living* (1992). Rohr defines the first form of poverty as "the poverty of sin, the poverty before conversion" (Ibid., 73). Whether or not we believe that we have been saved or that we have accepted Jesus Christ as our personal savior, clearly we are all sinners. If I consider myself no longer a sinner, then I become more God-like. As a sinner, I am never completely filled with God and, so, am wanting.

The second form of poverty discussed by Rohr involves awareness of the manner and extent to which we are oppressed. Oppression comes in all forms, not just financial impoverishment. Thus, oppression can be based on gender, ethnicity, sexual orientation, disability, or illness, such as AIDS. People in positions of power may not feel oppressed. However, many of us are victims of our own inner oppressor. Carl Jung observed: "What I do unto the least of my brothers, that I do unto Christ. But what if I should discover that the least among them all, the poorest of all the beggars, the most impudent of all the offenders, the very enemy himself—that all these are within me . . . ?" (1933, 235). No matter how rich or powerful, many of us harbor an inner accuser, which often surfaces in the form of perfectionism. The inner accuser is brutally oppressive indeed!

The third form of poverty consists of a simple, humble life. In taking an inventory of ourselves, we need to consider how much we trust God and our fellow human beings to meet our needs for, as Richard Foster notes, pursuing simplicity involves putting oneself in a dependent position in relationship to God and other people. In Twelve-Step terms,[2] our assessment of poverty would determine just how completely we have turned our lives and our wills over to the God of our understanding.

Finally, we each must address the poverty that arises out of our very real sense of powerlessness. Much in our lives is beyond our control. Many of us rage against or try to deny power impoverishment. Ultimately, be it through illness or loss, such denial comes crashing down upon us.

A key facet of the stance of simplicity, then, is to assess our own level of poverty in terms of: (1) our sinfulness; (2) the level of oppression in our lives, either at the external level or originating within our own inner accuser; (3) the degree in which we trust both God and persons to meet our needs; and (4) powerlessness.

In summary, we assume the stance of simplicity not by stripping naked in the town square but by (1) attending to quality and substance, not quantity and appearance; (2) by assessing our attitudes about "stuff" and about the poor; and (3) by looking inward to determine the different ways in which we may be internally poor.

Meditation: Have you met anyone similar to my Aunt Dorothy? What did you learn from them?

Action: Select any activity you do regularly and focus your attention on performing the task *well.*

Self-Discipline

As with many of the stances we explore here, the theme of self-discipline contains elements of paradox. Acquisition of self-discipline involves the repetition of certain actions that may ultimately benefit us but that we are disinclined to perform. Exercising regularly is one example. Exercise enhances self-esteem, improves health, alleviates depression. Yet starting a regular exercise program is something that many of us look forward to about as much as root canal work! The problem is that the reward is not immediate; the benefit not always obvious. Many people start an exercise program, then overexert themselves, either through injury or, by causing tremendous discomfort. Initial goals need to be reasonable and realistic in order to have any effect.

Another example of self-discipline is recovery within a Twelve-Step program. The road to good health is a very slow process, which can prove exceedingly long and frustrating for recovering alcoholics. During the early months of rehabilitation, clients must hang on to an idea and a promise that will sustain them.

The Twelve-Step program leads to the first element of self-discipline—the notion of attaining ultimate goals by developing new patterns of behavior through manageable steps. AA promotes the "one day at a time" method. Admittedly, some may find it simplistic. Even so, the concept reflects a common-sense approach; namely that major, complex goals are often best pursued through small, manageable steps. The delightedly irreverent film *What About Bob?* refers to it as "babystepping." Thus, the idea of not drinking for one day seems considerably easier than never having a drink again.

Sometimes we need to break down actions further in order to reach the first step. There are moments during the recovery process when one has to focus on not drinking for the next minute. Similarly, there are days when simply getting out of bed at a certain hour is exercise enough. *The Amateurs* (Halberstam 1986), a book that chronicles the struggles of young men trying to earn the right to compete in the Olympic rowing event, adopts such a minimalist approach to exercise and is, I think, quite helpful. One of the athletes describes the effort it took to even go to the river each morning to train. On some days his goal was to at least get to the boathouse. Consequently, as you pursue your own goal using small steps, you may at times need to tell yourself, "I've got to just make it to the boathouse."

What do boathouses and AA have to do with becoming a modern contemplative? Quite a bit, actually, because they both offer insights into achieving the stance of self-discipline. The joys of being a modern contemplative can only be gained by regular activities, or tasks, on both the inner and outer paths. The completion of these tasks (which we will be examining later) require self-discipline.

The stance of self-discipline is facilitated through ritual. Essentially rituals are set patterns of behavior performed in order to achieve a particular outcome. Typically we think of rituals in connection with religious activities, but rituals can be found in many other aspects of human behavior. Rituals ease our way. For example, when approaching the mysteries of the transpersonal, the divine, or the ineffable, we might be overwhelmed with fear. Rituals, however, prescribe certain behaviors that guide our way. Similarly, as Huston Smith notes, rituals assist us with confronting major life transitions, such as the death of loved ones (1991, 300).

Rituals also provide us with a set of behaviors that express a belief. Thus, if I, as a Catholic, make the sign of the cross, the ritual symbolizes the mystery of my participation in the Body of Christ. Rollo May defines ritual as the physical expression of myth but myth as understood in the classical sense of evoking mystery, not as it is currently used to indicate an illusion or mistaken idea (1991, 300).

In response to the question, How do I meditate?, ritual eases one's passage into the dimension of potent experience. The repetition of prescribed behaviors makes it possible to meditate in a consistent manner. Thus, if I sit in a straight-backed chair with my eyes closed, my hands resting on my thighs—palms open and turned upward—my breathing regulated (five in, hold for two counts, five out, hold two, and so forth), my passage to the world of the ineffable is made easier. By performing the same set of behaviors regularly, one can acquire the stance of self-discipline.

In summary, if we repeat particular acts over a period of time with the hope of achieving a specific outcome—be it sobriety, happiness, or physical fitness—we are acting on faith that the prescribed rituals will produce the desired outcome. Sometimes we must persist even in the face of doubt. Such persistence is the manifestation of the stance of self-discipline.

Meditation: If you knew you had a limited time to live, which activities would you undertake? In other words, think about those activities that you would put off until tomorrow.

Activity: Select one activity, such as meditation, journaling, or exercise. See if you can perform the same activity at the same time for two weeks.

Sensuality

The stance of sensuality will certainly jar the conceptions that many have of contemplatives as ascetics who fast and who generally try to deny their physical selves. Such contemplative models grew out of a worldview that divided persons into body and soul—with the greater emphasis placed on soul. I would argue, however, that a potentially potent pathway to the riches of the contemplative can be *through* the physical, not around it. The body need not be the contemplative's enemy.

Diane Ackerman's *A Natural History of the Senses* (1991) call us again and again to notice the world around us. I think it is impossible to read Ms. Ackerman's chapter on smell without at least waking up to the world of aromas and judgments we make based on particular scents. Consider your response to her list of smells encountered on a drive through farm country: " . . . manure, cut grass, honeysuckle, spearmint, wheat chaff, scallions, chicory, tar from the macadam road" (Ibid., 20).

In order to become more aware of one's body and grow into a stance of sensuality, contemplatives need to ask themselves a number of questions:

1. How often do you really taste what you eat and drink? Can you tell the difference between a glass of fresh stream water and something laced with chemicals? Do you gobble your food down because your mind is racing ahead in anticipation of the next meeting or the next date?
2. Do you like to sweat or are you embarrassed? Are you aware of the different types of sweating—that is, athletic sweating versus anxious sweating? Does the smell of sweat bother you?
3. Where do you typically experience stress in your body? Muscle tension? If so, where? Upset stomach? Headache?

4. What are your favorite pieces of music? What kind of music do you dislike?
5. How would you describe orgasm to a Martian who reproduces in an entirely different manner?

Sensuality also involves treating your body with respect. Thus, the path of the modern contemplative does not tolerate self-destructive attempts at self-nurturance. Nor, on the other hand, does it tolerate irresponsibility. Consider the following inventory of body respect:

1. Which of the following do you do on a regular basis: smoke? abuse alcohol? use mind-altering drugs? drink too much caffeine? What are the goals of these behavior patterns?
2. When do you overeat? Do you avoid food? Do you binge and purge?
3. To what extent do you engage in unsafe sex? Do you have multiple sex partners? If so, how long has it been since you were tested for the HIV virus?
4. What are five pleasurable nondestructive experiences in which you engage on a regular basis?
5. What sort of exercise do you perform? Are you compulsive about exercising?
6. Do you fail to take medication for a legitimate health problem? Conversely, do you medicate needlessly at the first sign of the sniffles?
7. Do you get an adequate amount of rest and sleep?

Our bodies and our senses are some of God's finest work. We are told, after all, that we are made in the image of God. A Catholic grade school education pounded into our heads that our bodies should be treated as temples of the Holy Ghost, a notion that actually had some far-reaching implications but, unfortunately, only was invoked to warn of the dangers of sex in general and masturbation in particular. When I think of the abuse I have done to my body in the past with alcohol or nicotine, when I eat poorly or neglect my asthma medication because I am "too busy," I become like the money changers desecrating the temple.

Our senses also serve as the gateways between ourselves and the rest of God's creation. By attending to the richness of information that passes through our senses, we pay homage and celebrate God. Further, through our senses we connect with much that can become objects for our contemplation.

Many forms of meditation suggest that we monitor our breathing more closely, which, quite obviously, involves attending to one's body. At this point, then, I would invite the reader to list the five senses. Try to attach a spiritual experience to each sense. Here is my own list, offered merely to stimulate thinking:

Smell: I have always found the type of incense used in Catholic churches during my formative years a "holy" fragrance. Only recently have I discovered that this aromatic substance is actually frankincense.

Touch: After completing my Fifth Step,[3] a priest-friend laid his hands on my shoulders and prayed for healing to occur. As he prayed, I felt a distinctive relaxing of my shoulder muscles, significant since I have asthma and also carry much of my tension there.

Taste: When I try to conjure up an image of unconditional love, I immediately remember the taste of my Aunt Peg's peanut butter cookies.

Sound: Several pieces of music allow me to glimpse the beyond. They include Pachelbel's Canon, Schubert's "Ave Maria," as sung by Pavarotti, and Daniel Schutte's "You Are Near," as sung by my friend Roland Guerrero.

Sight: I described an experience in my book *Encounters with Angels* (1992), in which my son Matthew and I had a profound encounter with a herd of deer. While driving away from an area deep within the Lincoln National Forest in southern New Mexico, we stopped to greet some twenty or so deer passing by. They did not bolt but simply stared at us with curiosity. A profound sense of connection occurred.

In reflecting upon my list, I find that sight, sound, and touch experiences came to mind fairly quickly, but I had to struggle for taste and smell images. Obviously there are aspects of the natural world that I am missing since I am apparently out of touch with my own sense of smell and taste.

Sensuality is an important stance because it directly points the contemplative *toward* the world rather than *away* from it.

Meditation: Using all five senses, think of experiences that address the dark side of reality. For example, for some reason I associate the smell of burning sulphur with evil.

Action: Allow five minutes for each sense, paying close attention to the stimulation that applies to each sense.

Detachment

I addressed the issue of detachment in my book *In Search of the Wounded Healer* (1990). Frequently detachment is misunderstood to be the same as indifference or, at least, a lack of feeling about something when, in reality, detachment has nothing to do with absence of feelings. I suspect the confusion derives from a misinterpretation of the Alanon[4] concept of detachment. In fact, Alanon encourages persons to "detach with love," which clearly means that detachment can and does involve feeling.

Detachment means being aware of our attempts to control the behavior of others as well as acknowledging our unhealthy abuse of power. Detachment does not mean indifference, nor does it mean inaction. Detachment permits one not to fear powerlessness and, at times, even to embrace it. However, before we can discover the power of powerlessness, we must break our need to control.

Several types of experiences offer insight into the way in which we attempt to control when confronted with a feeling of powerlessness. They include:

1. a crying baby in the middle of the night who refuses to be comforted;
2. transportation problems, delays, and missed connections;
3. being stuck in a traffic jam;
4. dealing with auto mechanics when one has little or no knowledge about the workings of a car.

At one time such experiences would have caused me to fly into rages (or, more correctly, tantrums)—demanding, bullying, and threatening. Thankfully, with the help of the Twelve-Step program, I am now able to control my temper.

Embracing powerlessness is more than simply tolerating inconveniences, however. It involves accepting a deep spiritual truth, which declares that out of brokenness and submission comes a greater power. We see this lesson reenacted in the *Star Wars* films through the sacrifice of Obiwan Kenobi. We see it in the nonviolence espoused by Gandhi and by Dr. Martin Luther King, Jr. We see it in stories of quiet persistent faith in the Nazi death camps. We see it in the Crucifixion story of Jesus Christ. But the power of powerlessness can only be discovered when we first control and then free ourselves from the *need* to control.

To achieve such a level of detachment, we must also become detached from certain expectations and desires, including the desire for prestige, success, recognition, or even our need to be unique. We must, therefore, examine that which drives us. It may be a drive for "stuff," but we are often equally driven by the desire for more elusive qualities. Thus we encounter overlapping between the stances of detachment and simplicity.

Detachment, then, introduces the aspiring modern contemplative to the important spiritual experiences of *emptying* and *letting go.* Emptying involves freeing oneself from psychological attachments; letting go involves freeing oneself from material and interpersonal attachments. If I am detached, I do not have to have prestige. I do not have to have a new car. I do not have to have a man or woman in my life. Although all these things are nice to have, the detached person is not driven by the inner demand to possess them.

The stance of detachment is enhanced when anonymity is embraced. My meditations, my journal work, my prayer are all private dialogues between myself and God. More important, they are done to enhance that relationship, not to attract attention to myself because of my holiness. Similarly, when my actions are done anonymously or within the anonymity of community, I am freed of the need to act because of an attachment to person, place, or thing.

Detachment is further manifested by a healthy self-effacing sense of humor. Contemplatives who take themselves too seriously are in real trouble. The contemplative who labels individual actions as "important," "relevant," or even "necessary" has lost the way. How many times have we seen protests where the faces of the protesters are frozen in anger? Protesters come closest to the essence of dissent when their behavior arises out of joyful community. Thankfully much of what I remember from the protests of the 1960s are the songs. "We Shall Overcome," "Blowin' in the Wind," and other songs recall passionate images of persons with arms linked together singing, even smiling.

The purpose of humor is not to laugh at the problems or at the suffering of others. Rather, humor helps us to stay detached from psychological attachments within ourselves. I have long felt that Jesus Christ laughed and joked a lot and that the disciples, humans that they were, took the whole enterprise too seriously, as reflected in the Gospels. The authors of the Gospels may have made the error of believing that Christ's sense of humor best be omitted. We all know that the shortest verse in the Bible is "Jesus wept" (John 11:35). Too bad the sadness wasn't balanced by the equally short but especially significant, "Jesus laughed."

Humor also offsets the likelihood of any contemplative becoming "addicted" to religion or God. Father Leo Booth has called our attention to this important phenomenon in his courageous book *When God Becomes a Drug* (1991). As Father Booth maintains, we can use religion or elements of religion in addictive ways, such as by trying to run away from various inner struggles through compulsive prayer, church work, scripture quoting, or other methods. When in the grip of religious addiction, persons are likely to become judgmental, swept up with a sense of specialness, and manifest many of the attachments described above. Thus we offset any addictive tendencies when we are able to laugh about religion, about sin, about churches, even about God. Sometimes jokes about God offend people, that is, people who take their religion and their God quite seriously. The God of my understanding, however, would laugh at the following:

A man fell off a mountain and was hanging onto a ledge, yelling for dear life. Finally, in desperation, he shouted in a loud voice, "Dear God, if you're up there, please save me!" The man's urgent appeal was met by a clap of thunder and a voice from high above: "Have faith, and let go of your grip on the ledge." The man paused a few seconds then asked, "Is there anyone else up there?"

In the same way we should be able to laugh about religion:

A rabbi, a minister, and a priest were discussing how each of them divided up the donation money between God and their respective institutions. The rabbi said, "I draw a big circle on the floor and throw all the money up in the air. What lands inside the circle is God's. The rest is for the synagogue." The minister replied, "I do the same thing only I draw a small circle." The priest laughed and said, "You guys have it all wrong. What I do is I throw the money up in the air and what God wants he has to catch!"

Meditation: If you were suddenly stripped of everything—possessions, roles, degrees, means of making a living—what would you miss most? (If the scenario seems improbable, recall the Jews of Nazi Germany or the Native Americans.)

Action: Tell a joke some time in the coming week.

Gratitude

You may have noticed by now that each of the stances places one in a certain position in life. Simplicity makes us respectful; self-discipline allows us consistency; sensuality makes us feel connected; detachment encourages us to embrace powerlessness. But the most central stance of the modern contemplative is gratitude.

Gratitude is not as simple as a thank you (although that certainly helps). Recall that we are discussing stances—approaches to life. Thus gratitude, as understood here, is not passive. Rather gratitude requires action—a going forth.

Brother David Steindl-Rast offers an excellent understanding of gratitude in his book, *Gratefulness: The Heart of Prayer* (1984, 20). He defines three aspects of the stance of gratitude: (1) recognition of the gift; (2) acknowledgment of the gift; and (3) joyful appreciation.

Recognition of the Gift

To recognize gift and blessing in one's life is not as easy as it seems. We can become distracted or anxious and focus too much attention on the past or the future. For this reason, recognition of the gift requires concentration. We must be alert to the presence of gift. In other words, we must notice that for which we are grateful.

Unfortunately many are grateful for a gift only when we almost lose it, or, more sadly, when we actually have lost it. Tragedy has a way of removing us from our shell. It is only when we step outside our shell that we can notice that which we treasure. I have had the misfortune of losing someone and realizing only later what a gift that person was in my life.

What would happen if we went through the day pausing frequently to reflect on those things or people who make us feel grateful?

Recognition involves an openness to wonder. Wonder, as we shall see in a later chapter, can be a doorway to mystical experience. To wonder is to be amazed, to be without words, to feel connected. It is one of those beautiful qualities of childhood that we somehow lose as we grow older. Some regain it. A fortunate few never lose it.

Have you ever grown something with a child? This activity can be effective schooling in wonderment. To see a child's excitement at the first green shoot, the first bud, the first fruits is to witness the essence of wonderment. But we cannot make wonder happen. We can only be ready to notice. Every time I go into the woods, I hope to encounter wildlife. Yet I cannot make it happen. When it does, even though I actively seek and hope for such encounters, there is an element of the unexpected. Perhaps that is the trick—to maintain the anticipation of being surprised, much like a child who anticipates the jack-in-the-box for the twentieth time. David Wolpe observes, "To a child, the mundane is a spectacle, and the everyday an amazement" (1990, 312). Such an attitude takes us into life—seeking, pausing, living. As the great naturalist John Muir once said, "This grand show is eternal. It is always sunrise somewhere" (1954, 312).

Acknowledgment of the Gift

It is not simply enough to notice. We must acknowledge as well. David Steindl-Rast challenges us to express gratitude without knowing the specific nature of the gift! In essence, we are deeply grateful before we even open the package. Such an attitude requires trust in the giver. And when the giver is God the stance of gratitude becomes even more challenging. Steindl-Rast notes, "God has a way of putting time bombs into pretty packages" (1984, 104–5). Or, to put it another way, "You'd better be careful what you pray for. You just might get it!"

Joyful Appreciation

Finally, our act of gratitude is complete when we reflect on what Steindl-Rast calls "joyful appreciation." Think for a moment of a gift you gave someone and the pleasure you felt when you witnessed the person enjoying the gift.

Like many people, I too tend to forget these experiences. I can lapse easily into self-pity, which Jerry Dollard suggests is the opposite of gratitude (1983, 8 and 12). I can become anxious about tomorrow or resentful about yesterday, two emotions that are incompatible with the stance of gratitude. Thankfully, great teachers keep crossing my path and help me to refocus and pay attention. A recent teacher was a young man whom I'll call Tom.

I met Tom at summer camp. One day we were on a hayride when a group of young people began to blare some loud music. Tom finally gave me a break from the music by playing a Garth Brooks song, which contained the lines "Sometimes I thank God for unanswered prayers" and "Some of God's greatest gifts are unanswered prayers." While the song was playing, Tom smiled and quietly noted how much he liked it. What made this such a heart-wrenching moment for me is that Tom has cancer and had recently come out of remission for the fourth time. Tom's humble manner and quiet ways taught me a lesson in humanity; for that, I am truly and deeply grateful.

Meditation: For one day, try to remember everything for which you are grateful.

Action: Let one person know what about them makes you grateful.

2

The Journey of the Modern Contemplative:

Journaling

2

If you can imagine the movement toward becoming a modern contemplative as a journey, then you can conceptualize the following chapters as a series of suggestions for what to pack.

One of the most important tools is a journal. Unfortunately most of us experience great difficulty with journaling. At first glance it may appear adolescent or trivial, like a diary. However a journal is more than a diary, for journaling not only explores our outer world but also our inner world. The real reason most people hesitate to jot down their daily thoughts is a fear that their interior world is barren and uninteresting. This is not true. Frequently even the most seemingly mundane existence can conceal a rich inner life. After all, when venturing into a desert one of the great delights is just how much can be found there.

Journaling

A journal helps in several ways. First it organizes the constant muddle going on in our heads. At one time or another, we have all experienced the frustration of gaining some new insight, a flash of realization, a glimpse of understanding, only to see it vanish forever.

A journal also can raise our spirits during moments when we feel defeated. It records changes that, on a day-by-day basis, can seem miniscule, so miniscule in fact that we aren't always aware of it. I recall, for instance, that during the summer when I had just quit drinking, I went back East to visit my family. One year later I returned. In the intervening year, I had tried to work on my bad temper but felt that I had gotten nowhere. However, during my second visit home, my father mentioned that he had been worried about me that previous summer—I had seemed so volatile and edgy—but that I had apparently calmed down considerably since then. Thus I was having some success controlling my temper, but, typically, I was the last to know!

Think of your journal as your secret garden, your cabin in the forest. It is intended to be only for you, a special place where you can spend quality time with yourself. Because it is a special place, you need to honor your journal by taking care of it and by keeping it private. Remember journals are only helpful when you are brutally honest with yourself. Therefore you may write about matters that would be hurtful or confusing if read by someone else. Just as others should respect your privacy, so, too, you must not tempt those around you by leaving your journal in an accessible place.

With that as a warning, now we can talk about different ways of working in your journal.

Events

Your journal is a place to meditate on moments in your life, great and small. Part of these meditations can include developing better awareness of your feelings. Thus you may find yourself writing about an ordinary workday, reflecting perhaps on your struggles with boredom or fear of failure. Or you may mention the joy of a small victory or of a lesson learned by contact with someone else. Of course, you may also find yourself writing about big events—perhaps grief over the loss of a loved one or fear regarding an upcoming job change. Practicing simple observation is also a worthwhile journal exercise.

Task: Make a list of the major stresses in your life over the past six months.

Attitudes and Values

A journal is a good place to explore attitudes or values. For example, you may find yourself writing about your feelings about money. Perhaps you will explore some facet of your ethical beliefs. You also may need to jot down thoughts regarding your religious tradition.

You may learn more about your attitudes and values by contrasting what you *say* your values are with what your behavior actually reflects. Essentially what you are trying to uncover here is the set of beliefs that underlie and guide your behavior in important areas of your life. It can be a humbling experience to uncover discrepancies between your stated beliefs and your behavior, but it is important to do so for it will help your growth as a modern contemplative immeasurably.

Task: If you were stranded on a desert island and could only take five books with you, which books would you bring along?

The Past

Your journal is the place to set down your story. Initially it helps to tell your tale simply by describing the details of the events in your life. As far as infancy and toddler years are concerned, you will probably need to rely upon the memory of others. If you are adopted, write about what you know of your natural parents as well as the circumstances of your adoption. Earliest memories, even if seemingly insignificant, can prove quite valuable, offering insight into set patterns of behavior.

If you find it hard to formulate a meaningful narrative, make a list of ten formative life experiences. These may be individual events such as marriage or the death of a loved one. On the other hand, they may involve more process events, such as regaining sobriety or, in the case of sexual orientation, coming out of the closet.

After writing your "autobiography," you may then want to read it over from time to time to discern any patterns or threads that may be running through your life. For example, I was recently doing journal work using as a framework some exercises suggested by Janice Brewi and Anne Brennan in their book *Celebrate Midlife* (1990, 71). The authors suggested writing about each decade of one's life, citing both victories and defeats. I detected several patterns of my own. The notion of priesthood had been very important to me for many years, yet I had never really confronted my decision not to enter the seminary. Nor had I explored that aspect of my personality that was (and still is) drawn to priestly qualities. From such reflection came the realization that a part of me is still "priestly." Better yet, these priestly inclinations can be carried out without actually being ordained! I also saw (again!) just how powerful an element alcohol had become for much of my life, always a useful reminder for a person in recovery.

Finally, using the journal as a road map of sorts, one's past can be examined to determine the existence of resentment toward others or shame toward oneself. Both emotional experiences, if left unexamined, can become toxic. For example, several years ago I used my journal to formulate a list of persons toward whom I held resentment. Prior to starting the exercise, I arrogantly assumed I might come up with only a handful of names. I had to stop writing after filling two columns of an entire page—a very humbling yet helpful experience.

Task: Make a list of your victories and defeats.

Gifts and Character Defects

Identifying your gifts and your flaws is possible in journaling. The defects may become apparent through your autobiographical work. If you have trouble identifying gifts, however, you may be either blinded by poor self-esteem or shielded by a front of false humility. Remember that truly humble people can see themselves as gifted. They just don't give themselves credit for the presence of the gift!

In acknowledging and celebrating ways in which you are gifted, perhaps you share in God's pleasure. Think of a time when you gave someone a gift, and they were moved or delighted upon opening it. Their response honored your gift. If you deny being gifted it is as if you invited God to your birthday party but didn't bother to open or acknowledge his gift.

Task: Make two lists, one of five moments in your life of which you are most proud and the other of five moments in your life that have been a source of great shame.

Dreams

First let me directly respond to those of you who are about to skip this section because you don't remember your dreams.

Not true. It's all a matter of paying attention. Simply place on your nightstand a pencil and a sheet of paper. Then try to retrieve some details—even a word will do—and jot it down before rising. After a few days of doing this, you will be recalling some of your dreams. I've focused on dreams with many people for fifteen years and have yet to meet anyone who doesn't recall something after making an effort. There was one fellow, for example, who insisted he couldn't remember anything. I suggested he try the above tips. He returned with a recalled dream two pages in length.

Dreams are a valuable resource to us in several ways:

1. Dreams mirror our hopes and fears, especially those of which we are consciously unaware. They can reflect issues within us to which we are consciously blind.
2. Dreams can reveal unresolved trauma from our past, experiences that we may have removed even from conscious memory.
3. Dreams can help us to acknowledge our inner re-sources—resources that we may not know exist. These resources, in turn, may resolve problems.
4. Dreams can offer words of encouragement about a par-ticular decision we have made.

When dealing with our dreams the secret is to recog-nize that the language of dreams is symbolic and that the symbols, in part, are unique. Suppose, for example, that two people dream about a horse. One person was raised on a farm and has good feelings toward horses. In such a case, the horse can symbolize the dreamer's natural strength. Now suppose that the other dreamer was thrown from a horse as a child and never was able to ride again. For that person the horse represents fears not faced or, perhaps, even the prospect of failure.

Your journal can be a place to work on your dreams. Some persons become so good at remembering dreams that they are able to write down five or six dreams a night and begin to feel overwhelmed. Annie Dillard once observed that nature often works in oversupply, providing an excess so that a given need will be met. Consequently a useful rule of thumb to remember is to make two assumptions about dreams: (1) that your inner self works on only three or four themes in your life at any one period of time and (2) that you don't have to work on every dream. If you remember many dreams, try to focus on those dreams that have an emotional impact, particularly nightmares or uncomfortable images or themes.

Finally remember that more often than not dreams are about inner reality, not the outer world. Thus if you dream about your spouse, it is more likely the dream is about something your spouse represents. Actions, too, have symbolic meaning. Fighting with someone may reflect an inner battle. It may even be a call for you to acknowledge your potential for violence (but hardly excuses a call from your unconscious to punch someone out). Later we will discuss ways of translating the symbols of your inner world.

Task: Record one dream over the coming week, even if it is only a dream fragment.

Dialogues

Carl Jung maintained that we do not have to confine the exploration of our unconscious to nighttime dreams. He also asserted that we could confront our inner self through *active imagination*. By that he meant using the gift of our imagination to interact with the contents of our unconscious. One way of doing this is to use a journal for imagined conversations or dialogues with your inner symbols. In order to do so, you must, first, avoid censoring what you hear and, second, refuse to question or doubt the veracity of the results.

Task: Write an imagined conversation between yourself and one of your favorite fictional characters. Ask that figure a question to help you get started. For example, if you chose Obiwan Kenobi of the *Star Wars* trilogy, your first question could be "What character traits might prevent me from becoming a Jedi warrior?"

A Place to Come to Know your Inner Artist

Often when I speak to a group of people, I ask anyone who is a "closet poet" to raise their hands. A closet poet is some-one who has written poems that they have never shared with another person. Typically at least half raise their hands.

A part of us longs to describe profound experiences in ways that do them honor. Often we strive to portray moments of wonder. In struggling to find words we may attempt poetry. Such explorations can be safely and productively done in one's journal. Other forms of expression, such as a drawing, may also be explored. Images are especially helpful when working with dream symbols.

The inner artist may also be present when trying to approach a particular problem in a new and reactive manner. In other words, you can use your journal for brainstorming. Gabrielle Rico's book, *Writing the Natural Way* (1983), offers a helpful framework for creative ideas.

Task: Finish this phrase in at least five different ways: "Death is like _____."

Lists

One friend who does excellent journal work helped me see the value of lists. Essentially lists focus on a central theme. Some examples of themes can include significant life events, influential books, greatest moments in baseball, and so forth. Not all lists have to be serious, however!

Task: Make a list of your choice of the five funniest movies.

Questions

At some point in our life, we may encounter questions posed by others that intrigue us. We may also encounter questions through workshops. Or they may simply be questions that life has posed to us. There may even be a question or questions that have become important to our spiritual journey. In my own case, the question Why does God allow senseless suffering? has been a central issue for some time.

Task: Make a list of questions that may explain your interest in this book.

Conclusion

Several good books offer more detailed guidance in the area of journaling. Morton Kelsey's *Adventure Inward* (1980) is especially recommended. Ira Progoff's series on journaling (1975) is also quite popular. A word of caution, however. When I first read Kelsey's book, I was very impressed by the depth and quality of his journaling as well as his determination—I was especially struck that he gets up during the middle of the night to jot things down. I resolved to follow a similar path.

One night I even made it to my desk. However, rather than making an entry, I subsequently succumbed to the sleep impulse, all the while thinking, "The spirit is willing but the flesh is oh so weak." I felt defeated. Before retiring for the evening, though, I did manage to enter some sketchy images in my journal, hoping that even such a minimal effort would be enough to tap into the necessary resources and inspire me during the middle of the night. What emerged, however, was an image of Christ walking with me outside a cabin. We looked through a window and saw Morton Kelsey sitting at a desk writing in his journal. Jesus turned to me and said "You're not Morton Kelsey. Don't try to be." Rationalization? I don't think so because that image freed me from trying to live up to somebody else's standard and allowed me to journal in a way that met my own needs. Had I insisted on journaling like Morton Kelsey, I do believe I would have given up long ago. Instead I journal when I can (and only occasionally during the middle of the night)!

3

The Journey of the Modern Contemplative:

Solitude

3

Becoming an everyday contemplative also requires that the aspiring seeker develop a capacity for solitude. However such solitude does not mean leaving one's daily routine behind, joining a monastery, or withdrawing to a retreat center or a cabin in the mountains. On the contrary, the modern contemplative needs to develop a capacity for solitude surrounded by skyscrapers and other symbols of urban existence.

Recall that the contemplative is one who quests. Initially the quest consists of a movement inward, in search of inner truth and growth, in search of a sense of connectedness ("What is my place?"), and, most definitely, in search of God. Such an inner journey requires emotional and spiritual movement away from the world. (Recall the stance of detachment.) Only then can we listen. Above all, a true modern-day contemplative must learn to listen.

Solitude

Solitude requires the ability to be alone. Many persons find being alone difficult, in part, because of the terror of hearing one's inner voice. (We will return to this point later.) Others have difficulty being alone because they feel guilty saying "No" or, at least, requesting others to respect their alone time. To take even fifteen minutes for oneself to write or to meditate means that, psychologically if not physically, one closes the door to others. Feeling the need to be alone is an emotion that is hard to explain, especially since a shut door is often interpreted as rejection. Thus the need for solitude requires ample communication with loved ones. It also involves trying to articulate to them the importance of this need and what it does and does not mean. To simply shut a door without communication is insensitive, if not downright arrogant.

Solitude should not be confused with loneliness. To be lonely is not only to miss human contact, it can also involve flight from one's inner self. Why would one want to flee from oneself? There are many reasons. Honest confrontation with one's interior world can be a humbling, even terrifying experience. I learned this lesson for myself several years ago when I attended a retreat-workshop at a Benedictine monastery in Pecos, New Mexico. I had been looking forward to the retreat for some time and had requested a private room to take advantage of the solitude. I arrived at my room, unpacked, and then became aware of the stony silence. I felt truly alone with myself. Almost immediately I felt the urge to drink! Drinking was a familiar form of escape that I had used for years. At that point, however, I had been sober for four years and did not wish to jeopardize my frail recovery. So instead I turned to my journal to explore the unexpected fear I had encountered in the face of meeting myself.

The inner path, then, requires courage because it involves facing oneself honestly. Further, it demands courage since it is likely that you will encounter the most dreaded and deadly obstacle of all—self-hatred. Only by facing this evil will experiences be based on true compassion.

Intentionally choosing discomfort goes against our grain. Jung noted, "When we must deal with problems, we instinctively refuse to try the way that leads through darkness and obscurity. We wish to hear only of unequivocal results and completely forget that these results can only be brought about when we have ventured into and emerged again from the darkness" (1933, 97). I encountered this tendency to seek "the easy way" in a dream I had a few years ago. In the dream, I journeyed to the center of the earth. But I did my traveling the carefree way—in an elevator. The dream seemed to suggest that I wished to achieve some basic truth but without doing the hard work.

To choose solitude is to choose a self-imposed exile where one leaves the comfortable and familiar behind, opting to dwell for a time in a strange land.

While exploring the inner life, we will encounter some troublesome waystations along the journey. They include confronting bigotry in our life, releasing what I call the Boo Radley within; defying the power of shame; meeting one's shadow; and, finally, struggling with self-hatred.

Lepers of Bigotry

The lepers of Christ's time were the outcasts. Fox, Kelsey, and others call them *anawim,* the forgotten ones. In our day, lepers are still ostracized, even though modern science has revealed the true nature of their disease. AIDS sufferers have become our modern-day lepers. I've often thought that, if and when Christ returns, he might work in a hospice for AIDS patients.

When we take the inner path, we confront two types of lepers: the leper of prejudice and the leper of shame.

Most people deny bigotry. We tend to think of bigots in a stereotypic manner, such as Bob Ewell, the villainous bigot of Harper Lee's *To Kill a Mockingbird* (1960) who assaulted children, or the gun-toting killer at the end of the film *Easy Rider.* The truth is that we view some element of society to be "different" and, therefore, because of fear or based on a sense of superiority, we avoid, dismiss, or belittle such groups. Thus the lepers in our lives may be proponents of women's rights, advocates of the men's movement, persons of a different sexual orientation (keep in mind, though, that gays can be just as bigoted toward straights) as well as the handicapped, the chronically ill, singles, childless people, poor people, rich people, military personnel, people who have never served in the military, and so on. The list is virtually endless.

Personally, I have struggled with several groups of "lepers." I have discovered, for example, that I react in a consistently negative manner toward persons of wealth and also persons in the military. With the former I rationalized my hostility by offering diatribes about the evils of capitalism. I attributed my aversion toward military types to my adherence to a philosophy of nonviolence. In fact each prejudice had its roots in my past. I had never made peace with my less-than-wealthy background or my own history of aggression and rigidity. I ran from myself and treated others as lepers.

Richard Rohr (1992) challenges us to pursue solidarity with people who are different from us. Many of us espouse compassion for the poor. But do we truly embrace them or simply settle for sending a check in the hopes that such gestures of largesse will make them go away? Do we promote social equality but protest when a halfway house is set up in our own backyard? Some forms of bigotry, then, may be less apparent, concealed by compassion except when that compassion demands a personal response.

One of my personal heroes is the Blessed Damien. Father Damien worked among the lepers of Molokai, even when they were abandoned by the church hierarchy. Thus Father Damien did not settle for visiting the island on a weekly basis. Rather he chose to live with them and embrace them. He eventually developed leprosy and became truly one with them.

The Power of Shame

The other leper whom we flee is the leper of shame. As counselor John Bradshaw notes in *Healing the Shame that Binds You* (1988), shame is a pervasive, negative emotion caused by a set of actions. In other words, this inner leper is the keeper of our secrets, our closet skeletons. It is the fear of the world discovering our deepest inner truths. This inner leper may consist of acts we once performed and now regret or some secret inner knowledge about ourself. In my workshops, I ask people who harbor secrets they do not want others to know about to raise their hands. Usually one half to three quarters do so!

In searching for the Boo Radley part of ourself, we first must remember that Boo Radley was the recluse in *To Kill a Mockingbird,* locked away by his father. The children of the story decide they will try to make Boo Radley come out of his house. Unknown to many, Boo comes bearing an important gift. Everyone has a bit of Boo Radley in them that, for various reasons, notably fear, remains bottled up inside but that also harbors secret gifts—the gift of knowledge, the gift of understanding, the gift of self-discovery. Your Boo Radley may be a hidden poet, or a person capable of assertiveness and principle, or, perhaps, a source of insights that you typically keep to yourself ("People will think I'm stupid!"). Sadly, if we keep our Boo Radleys locked up, they wither and die. My own Boo Radley, when I finally set him free, turned out to be a writer! But, at times, self-doubt and fear return and try to suppress him again.

Confronting our Shadow

Carl Jung would probably define the lepers and our inner Boo Radley as different manifestations of our shadow. Recall that the shadow reflects our need to hide those aspects of our personality and potential that we consider disgusting and unacceptable. But by "stuffing away," for example, our potential for violence, we actually give it more power. It can surface later as child abuse. Or we can project aspects of our shadow by aggressively condemning in others that which we fear most within ourselves.

One of the central elements of prejudice is shadow projection. In this dynamic, we meet one of the ways in which the inner journey brings us back into the world. By facing our own inner shadow and accepting it with humility, we remove the projections that we have thrust upon others. Matthew Fox defines projection as one face of sin: "Projection is the refusal to let be. To let others be different, be surprising, be themselves. This refusal to let be comes from an inner refusal to let oneself be, to be with oneself—the essential spiritual gift learned from solitude" (1983, 160).

The existence of the shadow suggests that we expend great energy trying to be perfect. Needless to say, we all fail. These failures produce that which is darkest within us, that which influences much of our behavior, that within which we avoid facing for fear it will ultimately destroy—self-hatred.

As with the word *bigot,* many of us shrink from the equally loaded word *self-hatred.* Most of us might admit, in a moment of reflection, that we don't always like ourselves but that we don't hate ourselves either. Self-hatred lurks behind the ongoing inner criticism that, for many, runs continuously throughout their lives. Self-hatred drives us away from enjoyment and comfort ("I don't deserve it.") Self-hatred drives us to be productive, to be "good enough." Self-hatred fires our addictions. Self-hatred blocks compassion for ourself. Still not sure? Consider, then, the following inventory of self-love. I love myself when:

1. I consistently take care of my health, get adequate rest, and avoid unnecessary stress;
2. I try to forgive myself and others, since resentments are toxic and unhealthy;

3. I am sensual;
4. I affirm myself on a daily basis;
5. I acknowledge the ways in which I am gifted;
6. I feel joy more often than I feel guilt;
7. I admit my faults honestly and without defensiveness;
8. I truly believe that God's love for me is unconditional.

If you agree with most of the above statements, my hunch is that you have done some healing work. Good for you!

Rabbi David Wolpe (1990, 2) observes that we do not emerge from this inner way unscathed. When we face that part of us that is dark and unpleasant, when we confront our secrets and shames, when we uncover our resentments, prejudices, and projections, it is a very humbling experience. It becomes impossible to feel superior to anyone.

A Sense of Renewal

But it is not just darkness and ugliness that we meet on the inner journey. We may also discover gifts or unlock valuable potential. We may come to look at ourselves in a new way. Ultimately we may hear the whisper of God for remember Jesus once said, "The kingdom of God is within you" (Luke 17:21).

What a dangerous statement that was! No wonder the church authorities wanted to destroy Jesus. If people really believed such a philosophy, church officials would be out of a job! "The kingdom of God is within you." The whole kingdom! Not just the back alleys. This potent statement places our spirituality on a par with Dorothy's plight in *The Wizard of Oz*. We search frantically for a great treasure, some solution to perplexing problems, only to find that for which we seek has been within us all along.

Out of our solitude can come a sense of renewal, albeit humble renewal. It is not sufficient to hoard the fruits of our solitude. Whatever we discover is meant to be shared.

4

The Journey of the Modern Contemplative:

Sacred Places

4

When I was young, I was always intrigued by the statement God made to Moses from within the burning bush: "Moses, you are walking on holy ground" (Exodus 3:5). Holy ground! What a powerful notion! A physical place where God could be found, which God had, in fact, blessed by his presence. I have spent a fair amount of time seeking such holy ground and only recently has it begun to dawn on me that, much like Dorothy in *The Wizard of Oz,* I have been seeking something that has been right beneath my own feet all along.

The concept of a sacred place is not limited to the idea, "It's where you find it!" Sacred places depend, in part, on what phase of the mystical movement is emphasized for, as we shall see, the movements of a modern contemplative do, at times, require solitude and isolation. Consequently, sacred space must be considered from two angles: (1) sacred place as a point of reflection and withdrawal and (2) sacred place as reverence toward all creation.

Sacred Places: Reflection and Withdrawal

Most religious traditions offer reflections about people who choose to live in solitude. Some leave the world as a way of finding God; others as a way of praying for the redemption of creation in general and us sinners in particular. In either case, such movement seems to be based on the notion that it becomes easier to hear the voice of God in quiet places. Sometimes we can find such places. More often, though, we have felt compelled to build them.

For some, sacred places are found in churches or syna-gogues. Church builders have attempted to accomplish two goals: (1) the creation of a respectful atmosphere where God's voice can be heard in solitude and quiet and (2) an artistic cre-ation that praises God through its physical beauty. More recently, church builders have also become concerned that our buildings address issues of physical comfort.

In contemporary society, however, churches and synagogues tend to be places where crowds gather. Hence the opportunities for quiet prayer are not always available.

A more recent development has been the creation of retreat centers. Religious retreats have been around for a long time but they have tended to center around specific groups, students in Catholic schools, for example. On the other hand, alternative centers try to respond to the needs of those who wish to have contemplative experiences. Such centers may present retreats around certain themes, may provide loosely structured contemplative experiences, or may simply welcome anyone who wishes to participate in the daily life of a contemplative community. However these centers are not always easily accessible. They tend also to reinforce the notion that contemplative and mystical experiences can only take place in particular settings. In finding our own sacred place, then, we may wish to consider Lawrence Kushner's rather pointed criticism of established religion: "Culture and organized religion conspire to trick us into believing that entrances to holiness are only at predicted times and prearranged places" (1990, 56).

At the same time, we tend to define major events in our lives in relationship to place. Ultimately, as Paul Tournier (1968) has observed, our identity uses place as an important component. "Where are you from? Where are you going? Where have you been?" The answers to such questions tell us much about ourselves, albeit somewhat superficially.

Pause now and recall the most potent spiritual experiences of your life. Keep in mind that such experiences need not be positive. Then take note of the setting of each experience. For purposes of illustration, I'll share a few of my own:

1. While serving at a Benediction service at a home for elderly nuns, I had a profound sense of God's presence and decided that I wanted to become a priest;
2. In the fall of 1990, I witnessed the death of a twenty-three-year-old woman. The sense of a powerful force

leaving her at the moment of departure has been impossible to capture with words;
3. I felt a tremendous mixture of shame, self-loathing, healing, and relief while completing my first Fifth Step through the sacrament of reconciliation.

As you can see from my list, only one of these experiences occurred in a church and only the first and the third incidents involved religious rituals. All three experiences are very important points along my own spiritual journey. Each, in significant ways, changed me. Further, the memory of these events is tied strongly to place.

If you were to seek out a sacred place, where would you go? Make a list. Some persons create their own sacred place, using it only for a specific spiritual purpose. Include such a creation on your list if it applies. Again, for purposes of illustration, I'll share my own list of sacred places:

1. The Tejas trail at Guadalupe National Park;
2. My herb garden;
3. The beach by the Pacific Ocean near Marina del Rey, California;
4. A Twelve-Step meeting place in El Paso, Texas.

How then can we identify our sacred places? An easy way is to list the fruits they bear for you. A sacred place is: (1) a place of comfort; (2) a place of belonging; (3) a place of encounter with the numinous; (4) a place of empowerment; and (5) a place of healing.

A Place of Comfort

Sacred places can calm and relax us. They are places where our breathing can become regulated and where muscle tension is due only to exertion, not to stress.

At the beach near Marina Del Rey, I will typically sit on a rock and listen to the waves breaking around me. My breathing always becomes deep and even. The only muscular tension is from the running I usually complete just before climbing the rock.

A Place of Belonging

Paul Tournier has articulated our need for a place of belonging, a sense of connectedness. This, too, identifies sacred place. It is a setting that evokes a sense of belonging, even if we are actually witnessing the place for the first time. Our sacred place gives us a sense of coming home.

There is a spot on the Tejas Trail that one can find after hiking up the mountainside. From this spot, you can look out over wide expanses of desert. It is breathtaking, a welcome rest after a strenuous climb. Whenever I'm there, it instills in me a deep sense of connection with the mountain, with the desert, and with my hiking companion.

A Place of Encounter with the Numinous

In sacred places, we may encounter the numinous, the ineffable, the face and voice of God. This is the essence of the burning bush. It is also the theme explored in Lawrence Kushner's powerful book *God Was in This Place and I, i Did Not Know It* (1992).

When I was at a retreat in Pecos, New Mexico, one morning after my run I walked around a small lake in the center of the retreat grounds and saw a spectacular sunrise. Finally, I passed another retreatant who smiled at me and remarked, "He did a good job this morning, didn't he?" God was in that place and, thankfully, I knew it!

A Place of Empowerment

Sacred places help us to gather power, a notion reflected beautifully in several Native-American traditions. Native-American culture tends to honor sacred places much more respectfully than others.

Healing or guiding spirits are often encountered in these sacred places. They may be areas where sacred healing herbs grow. They may be areas where people complete a "vision quest"—that is, the search for a central spiritual theme and guiding image. Gable Mountain in south central Washington state, Chimney Rock in the Siskiyou Mountains of Six Rivers

National Forest in California, and Kootenai Falls in Montana are all examples of sacred places. Unfortunately these and many other sites have also been areas coveted by various American industries and have been the focus of several legal battles.

A sacred place renews us, replenishes our energies, and occasionally gives us important insight. My herb garden is an empowering place for me. The invigorating aromas of rosemary, catnip, sage, and savory seem to dissolve my fatigue and fill me with spiritual spice and energy.

A Place of Healing

Finally, a sacred place is a place of healing, a place where we may expend pent-up emotion. It can also be a place where we learn of the value of mistakes, of wounds, by empathizing for others similarly wounded.

Sadly we have developed a tendency to associate spiritual matters to specific structures with the unfortunate consequence that we miss much of the sacred in daily life. We would do well to remember the Lakota Sioux's attitude about sacred places:

> Today they (the Lakota Sioux) formally and consciously reject permanent sacred architecture as suitable or as having any lasting significance. The transparency of the world of matter . . . precludes the thought that material permanence has very much to do with sacred space. Rather, by not being in a structure, one is in the sacred temple—templus—which is the world itself, with the actual dirt of the earth as the floor and the vast blue dome of the actual sky as the ceiling (Amiotte 1989, 253).

Reverence toward All

An attitude of reverence toward *all* creation is essential in creating sacred space. Several writers have turned our attention to this urgent need for reverence. Ecological theologian Thomas Berry (1988, 14) calls for "courtesy toward the earth." Nature, he reminds us, serves a significant revelatory function of the divine. Berry warns of the ultimate effect of loss of reverence: "We are losing splendid and intimate moments of divine presence. We are, perhaps, losing ourselves" (Ibid.). Indeed how can we, as a part of creation, treat the rest of creation with irreverence and disrespect without such negative energy turning back on ourselves? Scottish theologian Ian Bradley challenges us to view God as green, thereby manifesting his creation in an ongoing manner and inviting us to participate in—not to control—that creation. He places us in the midst of creation, not outside of it, with this beautiful metaphor: "It is almost as though every created being is an instrument in a cosmic orchestra, giving its own distinctive tune to the great symphony that is being played in response to the biddings of the unseen conductor" (1990, 39).

While it is imperative that reverence manifests itself in our attitudes toward ecological issues, we nonetheless need to carry this philosophy into the streets and skyscrapers. For the face and voice of God are there as well. Several of my own, most powerful spiritual experiences occurred in buildings—a home, a rectory, a Twelve-Step club—all human-made structures. As Abraham Heschel (Dresner 1990, 78) has suggested, religion tells us much about people's search for God. But they also speak of God's search for us. Will God not seek us out in our offices as well as our forests? It may be that God is, indeed, in my office, but as Jacob said, "I did not know it." Ultimately our sacred places reflect back something of ourselves that we have lost. Author Lawrence Kushner recalls discussing the contents of the ark of the covenant with a preschool class (1992, 10). One perceptive child made the observation that if someone were to look inside the ark, he or she would find a reflection of themselves!

5

The Journey of the Modern Contemplative:

Companions

5

It may seem contradictory to discuss both the need for solitude and the need for a companion when discussing the modern contemplative. Keep in mind, however, that the journey of the modern contemplative has a rhythm to it. Thus, there are moments apart as well as together; a going out and a return; a time to be alone and a time for sharing.

The journey is filled with danger. Recall the many reasons why people avoid solitude. One of the greatest dangers, oddly enough, can be arrogance, the idea that one has discovered all the inner and outer territory there is to chart. Such arrogance can indeed be blinding. Anyone who chooses to follow this path must heed the warning of Thomas Merton, "The most dangerous man in the world is the contemplative who is guided by nobody" (1961, 194).

In examining the need for a companion, then, we will take a closer look at why a companion is necessary and what to look for when seeking one.

Much of what we confront within ourselves is unpleasant, even frightening. The task of sharing one's dark side with another person is, therefore, terrifying in and of itself. If such sharing does not engender fear, then either the sharing has become superficial or your companion has lost the ability to challenge you. You may at this point wish to develop a list of qualities that you would desire in a person who is to be your companion. My own list includes the following qualities:

1. *A balance of sameness and difference.* I need a person similar enough to me so that I may have some confidence in being understood. Yet I also desire a companion who provides enough contrast so that I will have a chance to receive new information from a different perspective;
2. *A spiritual point of view.* This quality may seem obvious, given the nature of the journey we are discussing. What is important, however, is to keep in mind that

spirituality and religion are often different. Morton Kelsey has provided a series of excellent guidelines for determining which therapists employ a spiritual point of view (1986, 46). His observations can also apply to choosing a companion.

3. *A willingness to share his or her journey.* If my companion only listens to my struggles without sharing experiences, the relationship becomes unbalanced. If we each share and listen, we both can grow.

The contemplative may, in fact, draw on different companions at different points in time or for different phases of one's journey. Thus, to follow the metaphor, I may have a traveling companion but may also at times need to consult with someone who has more knowledge of, say, mountain climbing or fire-building. With this in mind, let's consider different types of companions we might employ along the way.

Spouse or Lover

Long-term, one-to-one relationships are some of the best sources of growth available. I'm going to use the term "marriage" to refer to such relationships, but I want to make clear that long-term committed gay relationships and long-term live-in relationships are also included.

Marriage challenges men and women at every level to share, to be vulnerable, and to learn to accept and forgive. All that can be toxic to relationships—resentment, disappointment, fear of abandonment—challenge marriages. Essentially we are challenged, through marriage, to learn to live with another person different from ourselves, a skill that is sadly lacking at every level of our society today.

I have been married for more than twenty years. My wife and I tied the knot at a young age and, in some ways, have grown up together. She has challenged me and especially has encouraged me to communicate better. My marriage has brought out the best and the worst in me. It has been both an exhilarating and a humbling experience. One thing has become clear to me. In order for it to work, I have to let this woman see a glimpse of my soul from time to time. It can be difficult and, occasionally, scary. But I also know that, if she were not my companion on much of my journey, I would have gotten lost in the woods a long time ago!

Friends

Many people have different kinds of friends—friends with whom we work, friends with whom we play, drinking and partying friends, friends who are neighbors. In many ways a friend can be the ideal journey companion.

I have been blessed with two very special traveling companions. Both are therapists. One is a few years older than me. We served in the military together and have helped each other through several rough patches, such as health problems, my own early recovery from alcoholism, loss and near loss, letting go of children. His professional perspective is different from mine in important ways, and he has never hesitated to challenge me when he sees fit. He has been a trusted companion on every major turn in my journey over the past fifteen years.

My other friend-companion is a few years younger but also brings important differences in perspective. He was, for many years, my running companion and, since we often exercised in the early morning, he became a valued dream partner. He moved away three years ago, and I still grieve the loss.

Mentors

Although the recent contemporary men's movement contains much that is silly, it has also helped to focus attention to a number of important areas. One area is the value of mentors in our lives. A mentor is an older person who informally teaches us how to function in a certain sector of society. Thus mentors can help adolescents move into adulthood. Mentors may include teachers, coaches, uncles, or aunts. Later, as we pursue a career, a mentor can help us attain competency and nurture our potential. At that stage in our life, mentors might include supervisors or more experienced colleagues. Even during middle age, one can have mentors. An older person can help us make the transition through a period fraught with inherent obstacles. Again a senior colleague may be helpful.

The concept of mentor is reflected in the AA emphasis on sponsorship. An AA sponsor is someone who has progressed significantly in the work of the Twelve-Step program and thus can offer guidance and support to "less sober" members. However sponsorship contains an important guideline—one does not tell another person what to do. AA sponsors simply share information that they consider important during the recovery process. The other person is not expected, nor obligated, to take the advice.

A man whom I considered a mentor died recently. He patiently answered my questions, gently offering guidance and, when necessary, even confronting me. His tender humor and intellectual rigor were standards that I could apply to my own life. Although our theoretical views eventually diverged, I continue to draw on his wisdom.

Therapists and Spiritual Directors

Therapists and spiritual directors are similar to professional guides, that is, persons who have some experience helping other travelers and who, through training and experience, have learned something about the "terrain." Such services, however, can often be expensive and better left to individual discretion. For this reason, seeking professional assistance is not emphasized in this book. The way of the modern contemplative must be made available to anyone who is interested.

As you probably have sensed by now, preparations for the journey of the modern contemplative are demanding in and of themselves. To embrace solitude, to develop skill in journaling, to create sacred space, to select and invest trust in a companion—none of these tasks are easy. And the journey is just beginning!

These comments are not meant to imply that therapists and other helping professionals have nothing to offer in this area.

In fact, mental health professionals have expressed an increasing acknowledgment of and abiding interest in matters spiritual. But there is also a great need for companionship and, thankfully, it usually comes at no charge.

6

The Movement of the Modern Contemplative

6

The rhythm of the ocean has long fascinated me—the rushing forward, the receding—all done in a steady, invariant manner: incoming waves bearing unseen treasures; outgoing waves cleansing the sand of clutter. Richard Rubenstein captures it so well: "God is the ocean and we are the waves . . . The waves are surface manifestations of the ocean. Our knowledge of the ocean is largely dependent on the way it manifests itself in the waves" (see Kushner 1992, 133–34). If this is true, then the Lord is surely a God of energy and movement, at times rushing in or pushing forward, receding to the point where we fear he will not return.

The journey of the modern contemplative is one of motion, a motion that, at times, can push us *into* the world and carry us *away*. It is a movement of constant leaving and returning. If we try to force ourselves into one particular movement, the rhythm is disrupted and discordance results. Thus modern contemplatives who remove themselves from the world are as one-sided and discordant as modern contemplatives who march in protest without taking time to appreciate solitude.

This chapter examines the four phases of the modern contemplative movement: the meditator, the contemplative, the mystic, and the prophet. The phases are not meant to be static. They are distinctive although they may occasionally overlap. The phases have been inspired by a variety of writers and experiences. Of particular importance are David Wolpe's concept of the *normal mystic* (1990, 2) and Susan B. Anthony's image of the *sidewalk contemplative* (1987).

Phase 1: Meditator

The actions of the meditator include but are not limited to formal meditation. In addition to passive meditation, the meditator also actively reflects and ponders a particular theme or image. The primary image is the wounded healer. During this meditation movement a journal would be especially useful.

As life has become more complex and stressful over the past few decades, meditation techniques have become more popular. Westerners have been flocking by the thousands to meditation workshops taught by Zen masters. Deep-muscle relaxation has become a valued tool in the counselor's medicine bag while meditation devices ranging from biofeedback machines to subliminal tapes have been developed.

Meditation for the modern contemplative accomplishes two very important forms of "letting go." First, we let go of the world for a period of time and go inside ourselves. Only then can the second, more difficult type of letting go be considered—the letting go of ego.

Ostensibly, meditation creates a quieting and soothing response. Indeed we must first become quiet if we are to hear anything of value that we can bring back to our communities. Often when I close my eyes, I notice that my breathing is shallow, that my stomach is fluttering with anxiety, and that certain muscles are tense. Such a physical state represents the inner noise that has built up over the course of hours, days, even weeks. Sometimes I also acknowledge a feeling that I have avoided or have not noticed. When the feeling is encountered on the path to solitude, I can no longer evade it. Thus, paradoxically, my own pathway to quiet often leads to an intensity of emotion.

Herbert Benson has done much to bring the benefits of quieting to our attention in his widely regarded book *The Relaxation Response* (1976). He suggests that four elements are necessary to achieve the relaxation response: (1) a quiet environment; (2) a mental device, such as a word or phrase to be repeated in a specific fashion over and over again; (3) a passive attitude; and (4) a comfortable position (Ibid., 27). The passive attitude reflects both cause and effect of the quieting and describes what will be referred to here as "quieting ego."

Who or what is ego? The term has taken on many meanings. In Freud's system of psychology, the ego is the part of our psyche that is caught in the middle of the battle between the *id* (primitive drives) and the *superego* (conscience). Later theorists, such as Harry Stack Sullivan, suggest ego serves more of an executive function of the psyche. In recovery circles, it is this executive function that must be quieted, since as the theory goes, our efforts to be "in control" actually make matters worse. Thus one often hears the tongue-in-cheek statement that ego stands for "Edging God Out." Ego, as used here, encompasses all these meanings. Ego refers to the inner element that provides order and direction in our lives and even at times attempts to achieve control over that which is uncontrollable. Ego is often represented in our dreams by one's self-image. If I dream that I am wrestling with a monster, for example, the dream may suggest an inner war between the conscious me and the shadow me.

When we approach quieting, we let go of our efforts to be in control. We also attempt to quiet the ongoing inner ego monologue that gives testimony to our hope, fear, and anger in day-to-day living. From a spiritual perspective, we must quiet ego so that we can better hear the voice of God within us. Some would even suggest that when we quiet our ego, we stop trying to *be* God!

Many of our finest religious thinkers have promoted letting go as a key to spiritual growth and good health. From mystics to modern Twelve Steppers, many people have spoken of the need to "let go and let God." However the journey inward can be terrifying. What we may encounter as we let go is not so much the reality of God as the extent of our fear, for all efforts to control people, places, and things are rooted in fear. The process of letting go, then, consists of three stages: (1) quieting the ego; (2) confronting the compulsions that prevent letting go; and (3) confronting the fears that provide the compulsion's roots.

Compulsion can refer to a quality of drivenness, a "must" or "have to" quality.[1] Richard Rohr (1992, 44) suggests three compulsions when trying to let go: the compulsion to be successful, the compulsion to be right, and the compulsion to be powerful. As we let go, we part with the need to be successful, even in meditating. We let go of any confining images of God that may shut God out. We become passive, even vulnerable. Typically I encounter intense feelings when I attempt to meditate—the fear of and resistance to the effects of letting go. I may be encountering my own shadow—that is, the part of me that values and seeks out power, sometimes at the expense of others. I may also encounter other images and feelings that frighten me. (Recall our discussion of solitude.) But I must have faith that these images will later become available for healing.

Herbert Benson, among others, has noted the physically healing effects of relaxation. In the same way, the process of letting go opens our emotions and spirit to healing. In fact, as we shall see shortly, healing may actually be a meditative path chosen by the meditator. In any case, the process of healing and the awarenesses and images that accompany healing are central to this phase.

A vast number of schools or theories of meditation exist. Some are secular, some are associated with various religions. Individuals on the path of the modern contemplative need to select an approach that feels compatible with their belief system. The approach must also accomplish the relaxation response, facilitate letting go, and enhance healing. Many books have been written in this area. Some are mentioned in the annotated bibliography.

Meditation encourages focused attention; indeed some forms of meditation, such as the rosary, Jesus prayer, transcendental meditation, and Tai Chi use focused attention as the primary technique. For many people, though, it is sufficient to simply focus on breathing.

When one has become quiet, the meditator may choose to remain in that calming state or may move into either prayer or healing imagery. However, in a quiet state, the meditator may desire some kind of dialogue with God or may simply want to listen to God's voice within. A reminder, though—healing imagery is somewhat more active.

Recent years have seen tremendous growth in the use of mental imagery to facilitate healing. Simonton Matthews-Simonton, and Creighton (1980) pioneered the use of imagery in the treatment of cancer while Bernard Segal (1986) has made the idea more widely accessible. For years, gestalt therapists[2] have used imagery to promote emotional healing. Linn, Fabricant, and Linn (1986) have incorporated quieting response, healing imagery, and prayer into effective approaches to healing.

Carl Jung was far ahead of his time in the development of the now-widely used technique of active imagination. In active imagination individuals take a dream symbol and consciously use their imagination to deepen understanding. For example, my description on p. 69 of using clay to better understand my dream is one example of active imagination.

When the meditator is quiet, the individual may shift attention to a particular theme in order to facilitate the healing process. The meditator may be guided by someone else or may be self-directed. (Recall, however, the importance of a companion for processing.) When the meditation is completed, the meditator may want to jot some reflections down in a journal.

Reflection is best done with a journal since thoughts tend to be fleeting. In the case of healing meditations, the meditator approaches not so much from a sense of health as a humble awareness of being wounded. Keeping in mind the entire movement of the modern contemplative, this awareness of and embracing of one's woundedness sets the stage for a genuine sense of connectedness and ensures that the words of the prophet are not spoken out of arrogance. No one expresses this concept more clearly than Henri Nouwen: "Making one's own wounds a source of healing . . . does not call for a sharing of superficial personal pains but for a constant willingness to see one's own pain and suffering as rising from the depth of the human condition which all men share" (1979, 88).

From one's meditations can come a sense of calmness, a quality that is a necessary foundation as one begins to reengage with the world. From meditation may also come deepened self-awareness, some of it can be quite humbling. But humble self-awareness can often bring peace.

Phase 2: The Contemplative

We tend to think of the contemplative as a monk or cloistered nun. Indeed, Evelyn Underhill contends that the contemplative evolved from the mystic (1970, 531). However, the view of the contemplative as it is undertaken here is much more grounded in experiences that are available to us all.

To contemplate something is simply to look at it or, more specifically, to behold, for "behold" suggests the possibility of an emotional response. To behold is not to act upon. It is to observe, to appreciate.

Most people have a capacity to contemplate. I have fond memories of watching my children engaged in some activity. I recall, for instance, the time when my daughter returned from a trip and gathered our four cats about her in the backyard, spending a few moments talking to and petting each of them. It was a special sight, but it would have been lost if I had tried to become involved. Other parents may relate to the contemplative moments of watching a sleeping infant or hearing the soft music of a baby breathing.

Nature teaches us that the contemplative approach can ensure glimpses of wildlife. Recently my son Ben and I were hiking in the Guadalupes and witnessed a herd of deer. Only by standing still and watching could we be assured that the deer would not bolt out of fear. The result was a prolonged contemplation of gentleness.

From this action of unobtrusive contemplation can come a deep appreciation. My contemplation of my daughter and her cats, for instance, gave me an entirely new appreciation for the joyful loving gentleness with which she approaches much of creation.

Those who have been married for any length of time contemplate one's spouse as they go about a particular task, sit quietly reading, or even as they sleep. These precious moments of contemplation can evoke a new or, at least, a renewed sense of not only appreciation but also of wonder. One need only observe the reaction of parents outside a newborn nursery station. Eventually you will see a new mom and dad contemplating their child, a tear rolling softly down their face. For someone else, the moment of wonder might come in the form of laughter.

These special moments of contemplation and wonder can only occur when the aspiring contemplative becomes skilled in the stance of detachment. To reiterate, the contemplative attempts simply to behold something, not to act upon it in any way. This act of beholding is intended to avert the need to control, to influence, or to direct. The act of beholding and the subsequent flood of emotion that it produces—be it joy or sorrow—constitutes the experience of the contemplative motion. Together, emotion and beholding can be understood as wonder. For anyone to fully understand and appreciate another person, place, or thing, you need to be able to behold. Matthew Fox calls it the capacity to "let be"—not indifference but rather the ability to allow a person, place, or thing to manifest itself without interference. This does not mean that we should not interact with the object of our contemplation. It only means that in our appreciative interaction, we do not try to change that which we contemplate.

Detaching is important to understand. When taken out of its overall context, detachment may appear to be inactive, passive, and, possibly, indifferent. The act of letting be, however, insures that the ultimate discernment of action is based on true appreciation and compassion. It is not self-serving.

To risk belaboring the point, let me reiterate that letting be is not simply leaving alone. On the contrary, letting be reflects a capacity to ". . . let others be different, be surprising, be themselves" (Fox 1983, 160). This ability allows one to let oneself be—which is, according to Fox, ". . . the essential spiritual gift of solitude" (Ibid.).

But not all contemplation is of the sublime or the beautiful variety. If we limit our contemplation to only "nice" feelings, our contemplative motion is incomplete. We also must contemplate the horrifying and the tragic.

Annie Dillard has observed that if one truly contemplates *all* of nature, one is, at times, frightened or saddened (1984). Thus, as modern contemplatives, we must be able to contemplate not only the forest in all its green beauty but also the forest ravaged by fire or destroyed by machines. We must be able to contemplate not only children at play but also children emotionally and physically scarred by cancer. We must contemplate all that is violent, vile, and abusive among people with full awareness that the same darkness resides within ourselves. Much of my own inner darkness I have uncovered during meditation. As a contemplative, I merely behold. Unfortunately the pervasive presence of television has brought darkness into our living rooms on a daily basis. How many of us were struck silent while beholding the following images:

1. the televised shootings of Lee Harvey Oswald or Robert F. Kennedy?
2. the explosion of the *Challenger* space shuttle?
3. a lone Chinese student trying to face down a tank in Tiananmen Square?
4. the hundreds of bodies in Jonestown, Guyana, or, more recently, the flames of the Davidian compound in Waco, Texas?

The list goes on.

Intense sadness can also accompany contemplation. I recently had such an experience while contemplating various panels of the AIDS Quilt, sponsored by the NAMES Project.[3] The magnitude of the senseless loss was truly overwhelming.

Abraham Heschel suggests that we need to develop a *will to wonder* (1951). The ability to wonder comes naturally to us, but we tend to subvert that will as we climb the ladder of success. When we are busy, we rarely stop to read, or write, or listen to poetry and, as Heschel says, ". . . poetry [is] the language of wonder" (Ibid., 36).

We also tap into a will to wonder when we act playful. Trees, for instance, can be a source of wonder not only when we behold a tree but when we *climb* one! When we play, we do not seek to change something or, if we do, the change exists only in our imagination. Persons who have difficulty playing miss a meaningful pathway to the divine. Alas, to play well you have to be able to take the risk of appearing silly.

Several years ago, I appeared in a theatrical version of C. S. Lewis's *The Lion, the Witch, and the Wardrobe* (1987). Since I played the role of the lion Aslan, I had to roar several times. As I prepared for the part, I thought to myself, "Surely I have within me the capacity to roar." I had trouble finding it, though, mainly because I was afraid to "let go" of my ego long enough to risk being silly. My fear was unfounded. When I roared one child, to the delight of both cast and audience, roared back. Playing is another way of letting go. Indeed one of the finest compliments I've ever been paid occurred when one of my clients, a six-year-old girl, told her mother that I was "kind of silly."

In assessing your sense of wonder and playfulness, consider the following tasks:

1. What have been the major experiences of wonder in your life? List five experiences of joyful wonder and five of horrified wonder.
2. How do you play? ("Adult" games such as golf do not count!) If you are not sure, go outside and see if you can roar.

Phase 3: The Mystic

Most of us equate mystics with saints, such as Teresa of Avila and therefore find the notion of mystic to be a foreign one. We believe that mystical experiences can only emerge from deep prayer, meditation, and visions. David Wolpe offers another version. He describes the *normal mystic* as someone who "looks at life as you and I know it, but with an acute eye, one that tracks the almost imperceptible or often overlooked suggestion of God in every corner, at each turn" (1990, 81). The mystic, then, like Henri Nouwen, is open to finding manifestations of God in *all creation*.

The mystic may sense, in the midst of cruelty and brutality, the distortion of God. While God may be manifest in all of us, our own brutality or indifference masks that presence. As Wolpe notes, "The betrayal of human dignity is more powerful and lamentable if one has a vision of what human beings might be. Ugliness is most awful to an eye practiced in viewing beauty" (Ibid., 89). Thus the second feature of the normal mystic is the capacity to see potential. Wolpe notes that normal mysticism constitutes a sort of double vision in which one sees, simultaneously, life as it is and life as it is meant to be. What a marvelous gift and marvelous corrective for cynicism! As a therapist, I am constantly barraged with the pain, tragedy, and ugliness of life. I must confront reality while, at the same time, entertain the potential of any given situation. Whatever the case, my assessment must always be grounded in realistic observation. Otherwise it is nothing more than naive idealism.

From sensing the presence of God, we are able to feel a connection, whether that connection is with an animal, an inanimate object, or another human being. Whenever a connection is made, we find the capacity for compassion. With compassion, we sense each other's pain, for when I experience a connection I, at some level, share pain. This type of mystical experience encompasses mind, heart, and spirit. At the same time, my ability for a compassionate connection is limited by my own circumstances. For example, I cannot fully grasp what it means to be a woman, an African American, or a person dying of AIDS. I cannot fully grasp what it is like to grow up in the inner city. Still, despite these differences, connections can be made.

I recall sitting at an AA meeting and wondering whether or not I belonged there. A person spoke who fit the stereotype of an alcoholic—he literally was picked up by the police while lying in the gutter. Yet when he spoke of the self-hatred he felt during his drinking days, I understood. The connection was made.

This last anecdote suggests the spontaneous quality of mystical experience. We cannot make compassionate connections at will—they tend to be exercises in intellect. Rather it is as if connections are made for us. The experience is almost instantaneous. All we can do is to try to make the experience possible through openness and vigilance. Perhaps the experience of connecting can be understood as a manifestation of God's grace, for certainly these mystical experiences would appear, to some, as grace-filled moments.

Dark Night of the Soul

The experiences we have described so far have been essentially positive and life-affirming ones. On the other hand, the Dark Night of the Soul experience allows us to truly appreciate our gifts by becoming painfully aware of absence—absence of love, absence of connection, absence of God. In the midst of joyous connection we suddenly are thrown into the pit!

When do we feel an absence of love in our lives? Initially most of us think of moments when we have been rejected or shut out, when we were forgotten. Thus experiencing the Dark

Night makes us realize how truly alone we are and leads to an awareness of those moments when we feel cut off, disconnected, with nowhere to belong. That awareness can bring a crippling sense of loneliness.

We also feel deeply unloved when we are the ones doing the rejecting. In essence we feel unloved when we behave in an unloving manner. The experience of the Dark Night involves a painful realization of how we react to others, whether stranger or loved one, with the opposite of love—indifference.

Ironically we sometimes feel an absence of connection when we are genuinely trying to make a connection. We feel misunderstood. Perhaps we try to discuss a profoundly positive experience yet find words inadequate to express our emotions. Or we may genuinely wish to grasp what someone else is trying to say but our efforts fall flat and may even cause irritation in the other person. The conversation lapses into a disappointed silence. In the midst of what should be a mystical experience, frustrated disconnection descends upon us.

We may experience God's absence in many ways. We may be too consumed with our own inner darkness to sense God's presence. We may feel abandoned by God in the midst of trouble. We may become exhausted in prayer and feel only anxiety, a lack of inner calm or comfort. We may be overwhelmed with intense doubt. In these cases, the exquisite sense of God's presence is gone. Where just a moment ago we felt afire with God's presence, now all that remains are cold ashes. The experience of the Dark Night of the Soul, however, is an essential facet of the mystic for without it, ego may dominate once again. The Dark Night insures humility, which is an essential element of the prophet experience. Without the Dark Night, a strong temptation surfaces to fashion oneself as special, privileged, even holy.

The experience of the mystic is filled with paradox: reality versus potential; connection versus loneliness; God's presence versus God's absence. But the ultimate benefit of the Dark Night can bring an even greater paradox. Only when we have experienced connection and compassion as well as the humility of separation and absence can we be capable of truly loving. As the gentle priest in Georges Bernanos's *The Diary of a Country Priest* says, " . . . if pride could die in us, the supreme grace would be to love oneself in all simplicity—as one would love any one of those who themselves have suffered and loved in Christ" (1954, 230).

The mystic, then, receives benefits that are not directly sought. In essence all that the modern contemplative can do is develop an open heart and an open mind.

A Loving Heart

I can offer no insight into the psychology of a loving heart, in part because love itself eludes definition. Glimpses of love appear in such books as Robert Johnson's *We: The Psychology of Romantic Love* (1983), Erich Fromm's classic *The Art of Loving* (1956), and Thornton Wilder's play *Our Town* (1938). I have learned from some truly impressive lovers—persons who have grasped the essence of a loving heart and reflected it back. I have also learned much from a visit to the NAMES Project quilt in San Francisco in which I felt the unseen presence of the many thousands who were and are still deeply loved and missed.

At this point I encourage you to compile a list of those people, places, and things that have taught you what you know about the art of loving. This list is an important gift for the modern contemplative.

Opening up one's heart in a loving way allows unexpected messengers to enter. For a loving connection is not limited only to one's friends and family. We are blessed with a sense of connection to *all* of God's creation. When connections are made, the result can be unsettling. As I write these words, for example, my beloved Guadalupe mountains are aflame, burning out of control, apparently as a result of an errant match from one of my fellow humans. I am deeply saddened.

From this sense of anguished connection will come a call to action, an invitation to protest, an urgency to involvement. For the mystic cannot sit idly by when something or someone that he or she deeply loves is threatened. In this way the modern contemplative will feel drawn away from the mystic life into a world filled with a sense of urgency.

Phase 4: The Prophet

One might expect that the prophet image would refer to predictions acquired by the modern contemplative during moments of mysticism. Not so! We adopt here the notion of prophet as understood by Matthew Fox, a notion that bears similarity to Susan B. Anthony's image of sidewalk contemplative, by which she means "the union of mysticism and revolution in one person" (1987, 136).

Recall that the movement of the modern contemplative is withdrawal, then return. In this way, the prophet returns for the world, not for personal gain or enrichment. The emergence of the prophet brings to mind the image of the Hero returning from a quest.

A few years back, I had the following dream: I am walking across a bridge, using a beautiful, immaculately polished walking stick. At the other end of the bridge is a man who challenges me to a fight, much like Little John challenging Robin Hood. I am willing to fight him but set down my stick because I do not wish to see it damaged.

I was stumped by this dream so I tried to sculpt the stick with clay. I also sculpted a hand holding the stick and, as I did this, I came in touch with the image of power. I realized the dream was chiding me, indicating that I tended to horde power by keeping my insights and realizations to myself and that I did not share for fear that they might get "damaged."

The modern contemplative confronts the fear of harm during the process of return. While it is true that we can be tempted to keep our realizations to ourselves—perhaps choosing to simply enjoy the peaceful feelings that they evoke—such a decision, though, is clearly selfish and a definite wrong turn from the contemplative path. As Carol Pearson states (1991, 57), the returning hero is faced with " . . . the challenging task of moving from the numinous to the work of day-to-day living—or better yet, integrating the uncommon and the ordinary. It is not the separate, transpersonal experience that ultimately matters, but how such experience informs the way we live our lives. That is what the return is about."

The crucial character trait that the prophet must possess is humility since the prophet will frequently address the problem of projection. Projection refers to the tendency to see one's deepest sinfulness in another and to attack the other person rather than attempting to heal oneself. In other words, we cannot address the projections of others until we confront our own limitations. Richard Rohr expresses the need for humility in this way: "You can't play the prophet until you've discovered in yourself what you accuse others of" (1992, 79).

In addition to humility the prophet is clearly called to deliver individual messages in a loving way. Thomas Merton observed that "In the long run, no one can show another error that is within him, unless the other is convinced that his critic first sees and loves the good that is within him" (1968, 69).

The prophet is faced with many challenges: (1) burn out and the need for discernment; (2) fame or notoriety; (3) rigidity and self-righteousness; (4) persecution; and (5) the shadow side of power. For these reasons, many aspiring modern contemplatives may content themselves by avoiding this phase altogether, trying to "cycle back" through the other more inner-directed phases. In my opinion, such a decision would be a mistake.

Burn out and the Need for Discernment

Without doubt, many prophets burn out. Men and women of goodwill become overwhelmed by the needs and demands of others. Often they try to meet all these needs and end up depressed, discouraged, physically ill, even addicted. For this reason, modern contemplatives have a great need for discernment as they move to act. It may be that the direction of the modern contemplative is clearly stated during the course of the inner journey. More often, though, the modern contemplative has only a general sense of service. Specific areas and means of intervention require discernment. In short the modern contemplative is called to discern when to say "Yes" and when to say "No."

This process of discernment requires a level of awareness regarding one's own gifts. An individual may be a skilled organizer, another may be a wonderful public speaker. Subsequently such awareness will narrow the possible means in which one will take action. In the same vein, the modern contemplative needs to be aware of deficiencies and be prepared to say no if invited to perform a task for which he or she lacks expertise.

Many well-meaning prophets feel drawn to help the poor and so may set out for the inner city or to a Third World country where the needs are vast and the problems are complex. In an effort to be of service, the prophet may soon feel overwhelmed and defeated by the sheer magnitude of the problems. This anxiety can be further intensified if the prophet lacks the capacity to gently say no.

One's recognition of individual wounds and the related healing process can also help during discernment. Clearly such discernment guides the millions of people who are involved in service through Twelve-Step programs. It is even the guiding, if unconscious, force leading many young persons into counseling and ministry. Sadly many prophets who try to "push through" burn out, teeter at the edge of despair. This condition is ironic since it is such despair that the prophet hopes to dispel in others.

Fame

Some prophets not only communicate their message effectively but also become famous or powerful in the process. Numerous examples of famous modern-day prophets include Dr. Martin Luther King, Jr., Caesar Chavez, Oscar Romero, Mother Teresa, Bill W., Larry Kramer, and Dorothy Day.[4] Fame can become a mixed blessing. Although fame may open doors that would otherwise remain closed, particularly within the political arena, it can also obscure the prophetic vision. The danger of fame underlies the concept of anonymity in programs such as AA. In fact, in AA one can find not only an historical testimony to the inherent dangers of fame but also the remarkable decision of Bill W. (1988, 205–9) to choose "principle over personality" when he declined an honorary degree offered to him by Yale University.

This conflictual element of fame is especially troubling for the modern-day prophet since fame's concomitant companion is power, and power is needed by the *anawim* (forgotten ones) for whom the prophet may speak. The prophet must remember two things: (1) that one person does not liberate another (we can only *create* opportunities in which it becomes possible for an individual to achieve liberation) and (2) the stance of simplicity can help insure that the prophet does not fall victim to the very wealth and power from which he or she may use to help others find liberation.

Rigidity and Self-Righteousness

Sadly the best examples of prophecy turned rigid are found in organized religions. The tenets of Christianity, for instance, often have been used to justify discrimination, the acquisition of wealth even when such acquisition causes suffering to others, and the physical abuse of spouses and children. A rigid point of view requires an enemy to sustain itself. Such "enemies" of Christianity have included and continue to include rival churches, Jews, communists, feminists, homosexuals, and liberation theologians. John Shelby Spong in his courageous work *Rescuing the Bible from Fundamentalism* (1992) explores the topic of rigidity in the Church at length while a chilling indicator of the "us versus them" philosophy is found in Phillip Berman's interview (1990, 110) of Jim Farrands, the Grand Wizard of the Ku Klux Klan. At one point during the interview, Farrands made the following statement that caused me, a Catholic, to cringe: "I was raised as a Catholic, and a lot of people think that the Klan doesn't admit Catholics, but we do. In the Northeast, Catholics are the majority in the Ku Klux Klan."

Persecution

The above discussion of the dangers of rigidity points to the next challenge facing the modern contemplative—persecution. Persecution may come in the form of verbal attacks, either of the sophisticated or unsophisticated variety. Sometimes though such verbal assaults can appear inadvertently as a compliment. For instance, one of the nicest compliments I was ever paid came during an imagery exercise using Psalm 23 in which I substituted "she" wherever God was referred to as "he." During the discussion, one man accused me of being a feminist. While he didn't intend it as a compliment, I was pleased to know that I was on the right track!

Verbal attacks, however, can be far more hurtful. Some of the ugliest words are words of persecution, such as "nigger," "faggot," or "bitch." Even neutral words such as "Jew," "gringo," or "humanist" can be used in a disparaging way.

Finally, persecution can take the form of violence, even murder. Some of our modern-day prophets have been assassinated. Others who have spoken out against injustice or have served as missionaries in dangerous areas have been beaten, tortured, and raped. Some of these victims' names never reach the front pages of our newspapers. Other prophets such as South Africa's Nelson Mandela—now South Africa's president—have been imprisoned. Persecution then is a very real, very terrifying ordeal.

The threat of persecution can elicit fear within the modern contemplative. Yet the modern contemplative needs to understand that fear is merely an emotion and therefore normal. One should not judge oneself harshly because of feeling fear in the face of deciding to act. Fear only becomes a problem if it makes the decision for you. I have dealt with courageous people who judged themselves too harshly because they felt a moment of terror. One man in particular doubted the strength of his faith because he experienced fear. How sad! Courage can only exist when fear is also present.

The Reality of Anger and Power

Much of the growth of the modern contemplative has focused on emptying, letting go, accepting powerlessness. How well does this prepare the prophet who may enter the domain of politics, a domain in which power holds center stage and injustice often speaks loudly? Power can be a troublesome notion for the modern contemplative and even more alluring than the prospect of fame. Remember, though, that much of the power of the modern contemplative evolves from the original acceptance of powerlessness and subsequent growth to a deeper sense of connection. In essence the modern contemplative exchanges one form of power for another. He or she exchanges the power of might makes right for the power of the meek shall inherit the earth. Thus a primary tool for intervening is the political strategy of passive resistance. Those who resist passively are not so much interested in being proven right. Rather their main goal is to change the existing system. This concept of power has a parallel in the field of family therapy. The school of therapy known as Brief Strategic Therapy encourages the therapist to interfere with problem solving. This may mean blocking current solutions so that better ones can take their place. So, too, with the prophet. The prophet interferes with current solutions so that alternatives may be considered.

But what of anger? Is not protest necessary at times when the modern contemplative witnesses inhumane treatment of other participants in God's creation? Yes there is room for, even a need for anger. But the modern contemplative must balance anger with constant vigilance against self-righteousness.

The modern contemplative must also strive to listen, even in the midst of anger. For when two persons stop listening polarization occurs. At the same time, the modern contemplative cannot be naive. Not all persons—certainly not all persons in a position of power—have good intentions. Some people clearly perpetrate evil in the name of power or principle. Evil and injustice need to be confronted. The spirit of passive resistance, however, insures that the confrontation be done respectfully and without violence. Central to this concept of power is the notion that authority that cannot permit itself to be questioned and resisted is really an authority based on fear. A healthy, God-based authority welcomes dissension. William Safire said it best: " . . . in the exercise of any kind of power, the best way to create a constituency of the devout is to stimulate the creativity of the defiant" (1992, *xxiii*).

From a personal perspective, the realization of the power that comes from embracing powerlessness came in a somewhat different way. I inherently knew that "powerlessness" was an important concept in the Twelve-Step recovery program. It was only after several years of therapy that I noticed that Step Eleven included the word *power*. While Step One encouraged me "to admit that I was powerless over alcohol," Step Eleven allowed me to pray for knowledge of God's will "and the power to carry that out." The path to true power involved first discarding what I thought was my own power, then accepting a new understanding of power. But to be truly "reborn," I had to relinquish the pseudo-power, with no certainty that anything would take its place. In retrospect I now see that only if we embrace powerlessness for what it is can we understand the kind of power that is personified by Gandhi, by Dr. King, and by Jesus on the cross.

One final observation is necessary regarding the prophet stance of the modern contemplative. The concept of "should" has no place in the type of action required. Recall that one facet of the discernment process is to determine one's gifts. Thus the action of the prophet may not appear "radical" in the traditional sense of protest (although, for some, protest will be an action of choice). Thomas Merton wrote during a time before social justice became a dynamic spiritual focus. Larry Kramer participates in protest marches but his actions that have the most impact are the plays he has written about the AIDS epidemic. For other people who choose to live simple lives, the actions may simply involve loving acts in one's own neighborhood. Too often many potential modern contemplatives feel unnecessary guilt because they do not visit impoverished countries or operate soup kitchens or participate in Greenpeace missions (all valuable actions to be sure). Consequently these potential modern contemplatives take no action at all.

The phases of meditator, contemplative, mystic, and prophet are not stages or levels. They are simply still photographs of an ongoing, overlapping process of growth and movement. There is, however, a fifth image that, in many ways, captures the essence of the various phases. The modern contemplative may be most thoroughly reflected in the image of the clown.

The Clown

Whom do you think of when you hear the word *clown*? Emmet Kelly of the sad face and baggy pants? Harpo Marx with his little horn? Charlie Chaplin's tramp? I, too, think of these great clowns, but the first character that comes to my mind is Jackie Gleason's the Poor Soul. The Poor Soul was a harmless man who said very little and often tried to be friendly or helpful but would often make a mess of things. At the end of each routine, he would pat his hands together, shrug his shoulders, and walk off. The character made me both laugh and cry, as good clowns often do.

Ann and Barry Ulanov provide an extensive psychological study of the clown image in *The Witch and the Clown* (1987, 204). Especially relevant is their discussion of the clown as a pathway to spiritual freedom: "The clown is a fool, but often a positive fool who shows us the folly of our human ways when we take them as ultimate values. The fool makes us laugh even at our most sacred notions and beliefs, thus leaving open a space for us in which something beyond our ego-constructions can enter." They summarize what might also be viewed as the finest achievement of the modern contemplative: "The clown pokes holes in our universe. By means of those holes a larger sun may shine through, visions of larger galaxies may be glimpsed. In the true meaning of a sense of humor, a clown may restore our sense of proportion" (Ibid.).

An interesting parallel to the Ulanovs' observations is found in Mark Stolzenberg's book *Be a Clown!* (1989, 150). "A good clown shares warmth, love, and insights into the human condition with an audience," he writes. "Clowns often criticize, mock, and satirize established institutions and authority figures in ways which are socially acceptable." Stolzenberg also makes the telling observation that "A clown must have a strong center. This frees you to take risks and be a little outrageous" (Ibid.).

Using the above observations we can see some striking parallels between the clown and the modern contemplative:

1. **Meditator**
   Clearly Stolzenberg's comment about a strong center reflects the focus of the meditator.
2. **Contemplative**
   The strong center gives rise to the ability to let go and take risks. A good clown, then, has made peace with control as an issue.
3. **Mystic**
   The clown's routines arise out of a sense of connectedness with others, especially with the *anawim*.

4. **Prophet**

What better definition of the prophet than a person who "pokes holes" in our worldview so that light might shine through?

To become a modern contemplative must we foresake the forest for white greasepaint and baggy paints? Do we discard our placards and turn instead to pantomime? Hardly. At the very least, though, the image of the clown can remind us that sometimes we can accomplish more when we avoid what Watzlawick, Beavin, and Jackson call "escalating power struggles" (1967). In other words, sometimes we can "poke holes" more easily when we are not focused on winning an argument or scoring points.

We tend to tolerate irreverence in clowns. We tend to give clowns permission to mock our most sacred beliefs. We tend to laugh rather than take offense. Thus the clown is in a particularly powerful position to nudge us toward change. We may tune out politicians—even preachers—but typically we will listen to a good clown.

7

Messengers and Trailheads

7

Having developed an overview of the journey to become a modern contemplative, you may now be wondering where to find the trailhead; that is, the point at which the trail begins. What follows are some suggestions of different starting points at different phases of the journey. The most sensible place to begin is to take a personal inventory of your needs to determine what significant road signs have guided you on your journey thus far.

Recently I have come across several edited anthologies of sacred writings from different cultures. Typically these collections include excerpts from the Bible, the Koran, and the writings of Lao Tsu, among others. Inspired by these ancient thoughts, I decided to define my own set of sacred writings. But rather than merely listing those writings that should be included, I thought about works that have made a great impact on my own psychospiritual journey—works that have helped me formulate my understanding of a Higher Power, works that have given me a glimpse of the face of God.

As I compiled my list, I realized that music speaks strongly to me of God. So, too, do certain poems. Not all of the works were specifically about God. Some addressed broader themes, such as the great mysteries of life and death. Other works merely touched my soul for reasons unknown.

I offer my list not because I think it is a model. In fact many of the works are well-known and hardly unique. Rather I hope the list helps to identify foundations that have sustained you thus far. They may offer you directions for meditation. They may simply comfort you in moments of brokenness. When I contemplate my own list, I feel joy, gratitude, and a sense of wonder at these beautiful artistic creations.

Sacred Writings List

The four Gospels*
Parts of Isaiah, especially chapters 2, 35, and 40
Psalms 23, 90, 91, and 139
Our Town by Thornton Wilder (1938)
"The Road Not Taken" by Robert Frost (1979)
The Wounded Healer by Henri Nouwen (1979)
Honey from the Rock by Lawrence Kushner, especially his poem on puzzle pieces (1990, 69–70)
"Do Not Go Gentle into that Good Night" by Dylan Thomas (1957)
Pachelbel's Canon
Schubert's "Ave Maria"
Daniel Shutte's "You Are Near"
Diary of a Country Priest by Georges Bernanos (1954)
May I Hate God? by Pierre Wolff (1979)
"We Agnostics" from Alcoholics Anonymous (1976)
The Story of Ferdinand the Bull by Munro Leaf (1946)

As I share my list, I feel a strong sense of vulnerability, for my list tells much about my inner world and my journey thus far. Some may judge me—an admittedly scary thought. Yet I also feel blessed for I can recall the guidance and comfort I received. Frost's poem, for instance, has been a reference point for me when I have made a decision only to be haunted by regrets. It has helped to dispel any doubts. Daniel Shutte's hymn, based on Psalm 139, has sustained me in times of deep sadness. *May I Hate God?* by Pierre Wolff has helped me to accept the occasional anger I have toward God. These works have been invaluable resources and have comforted me in immeasurable ways. Better yet, there are other works waiting to be discovered that will be added to my list—an exciting prospect that I look forward to with great anticipation.

Take some time, then, to compose your own list. Place it in a part of your journal where there will be space for additions. You may want to write down any thoughts on the significance of each entry in your own journey.

---

* I favor *The Living Bible* (Wheaton, Ill.: Tyndale House, 1971).

Trailheads for Meditators

The phase of the meditator requires an approach to quieting. As noted in chapter 6, numerous approaches and techniques can apply, some emphasizing physical relaxation, some imagery, and some a narrowing of attention.

Once the meditator has acquired skill at quieting, an inner trailhead is needed. Chapter 2 offers possibilities for journal topics. The following are specific examples of how one might begin this inward journey.

Works of Art

One obvious starting point for meditation is with any of the selections listed in your sacred works. Select one and write about what strikes you the most. *Our Town,* for example, has always been a treasured starting point for me, especially the third act in which Emily has died and is given the opportunity to return to the world of the living for one day. She chooses her twelfth birthday. Very quickly, though, she realizes her mistake. For she has returned with the knowledge of everything that followed. Desperately, she tries to have everyone look at one another, if just for one moment. But her family, not knowing the future, goes about their day-to-day activities. Emily can't bear it: "I can't. I can't go on. It goes so fast. We don't have time to look at one another . . . I didn't realize. So all that was going on and we never noticed." After saying her goodbyes, she asks the stage manager "Do any human beings ever realize life while they live it? every, every minute?" (Wilder 1938, 99–100)

Do we? Do you? No, I am neither poet nor saint. I can let fear distract me. I can become too self-absorbed. I can even lose a given moment by trying too hard to hold onto it. To truly cherish a moment we must accept that we will grieve after it has past. I felt much the same way on a Christmas night some years ago when my children were small or, during a camping trip, when we would descend from the mountains to the hot desert and then make the return journey home.

Is there anything that helps us truly cherish a moment, anything that helps us to just look at one another? The stance of gratitude offers one possibility. If we approach our day gratefully, each moment can be seen as gift. Gratitude can help us find a balance between past and present.

Let's look at it from a personal perspective. Using the meditation approach, I simply watch as my wife cooks our meal (contemplative), feeling very grateful that she is my companion (mystic). But it is not enough for me just to feel it. It matters to me (and, I think, to her) if I tell her (prophet). She is a little surprised when I do that. While she is used to my idiosyncracies, receiving expressions of gratitude from me is a rare thing.

Obviously this movement does not change the world, but it can affect our personal life. The movement of the modern contemplative ought to fill our entire existence, not just our public face.

Other trailheads I have encountered include:

1. *Moments of intense emotion for which I cannot account* (such as irritation with a client who has not been obviously unpleasant with me and other, similar situations). These experiences, when they occur, usually reflect my own unconscious issues or my need to control.

2. *My successes and failures.* Examples that have appeared in my journal include thoughts and feelings about conflicts with colleagues because of my own lack of management skill, or, on the positive side, thoughts and feelings after presenting a successful workshop.

3. *A specific dream.* Dreams have long been potent trailheads for my meditations. I have offered some examples in this and other works. I once had a dream about a conflict I was having with someone. The dream confronted me with two realities: I was feeling sorry for myself (the dream setting was near a garbage dump, suggesting that I was feeling "dumped on") and that I was on the point of deciding to avoid an issue (the person in the dream kept trying to talk to me and I refused to answer). The dream provoked some humbling journal entries as well as a letter to the person involved.

4. *A chance encounter with someone who stays in my mind.* This encounter may even be a fictional person, such as a character in a book or film. Recent examples

in my own life include a young cancer victim as he stood next to a hummingbird feeder, his finger extended near the mouth of the feeder. When I asked him what he was doing, he said quite simply, "If you wait long enough, a hummingbird will land on your finger." That event has haunted me and has been the focus of many meditations. At the fictional level, I find my thoughts at the moment turning to Forrest Gump!

At this point, you might consider making a list of your own trailheads.

Teachers for Meditators

The elderly are among the finest meditators. One of my fondest memories are of my maternal grandfather sitting pensively beneath a cherry tree in a rocking chair next to his garage, smoking a pipe. At the time, I found his passive behavior rather puzzling, for I was more interested in running through a nearby field or plundering his raspberry patch. In retrospect I now see that some of this "action" was what the psychologists call "life review." He had a long and full life, having raised his family of seven children after losing his wife in the flu epidemic of 1919. Now was the time to sit back, relax, and ponder.

I also recall my great Aunt Margaret, a woman who was liberated long before it was fashionable. She, being more extroverted than my grandfather, would share her memories and reflections. I remember one conversation in particular when she, nearly ninety-years old at the time, asked me what I thought of the Vietnam war, which was then currently raging. I told her that I thought it was not good. She nodded in agreement, then slowly shook her head and simply said, "So many young men . . .," her voice trailing off. She who had lived through four wars had seen enough of death and violence—a treasured lesson from one who had become an expert in the art of meditation. I might add that the subjects of her meditations were not always quite so serious. I recall, for instance, when she mentioned the time she saw Babe Ruth play baseball. Fan that I was, I asked for her impressions. She only said, "Clumsiest man I've ever seen!"

In my workshops, I often ask participants to name someone who they feel loves them unconditionally. Many people reply, unequivocally, their grandparents. My mother often says "Parenting is a responsibility. *Grand*parenting is a luxury." Perhaps grandparents are less concerned about proper or socially acceptable behavior with children.

Trailheads for Contemplatives

When we move into a contemplative state, we may need to set down our journals and pens so that we simply might look, listen, taste, touch, and smell. To become more fully aware of my contemplative side, for example, I make from time to time lists of certain events or activities that I enjoy. The following is a sampling of my choice of great moments in baseball:

1. Willie Mays's catch of Vic Wertz's mammoth drive;
2. Bill Mazeroski's World Series-winning home run against the New York Yankees in 1960;
3. Carlton Fisk's game-winning home run in game six of the 1975 World Series.

These are wondrous moments of athletic skill and human drama. How do I honor such moments? Describing the event and my feelings of amazement always falls short. Words fail to effectively capture the power except, perhaps, when those words are in the form of poetry.

I noted in chapter 2 that a journal can be a place to come to know one's inner artist. It is here where we can honor moments of wonder with the magic of poetry.

A Mini-Course on Writing Poems

If you are a published or an accomplished poet, this section may seem unnecessary. However most aspiring modern contemplatives may find it hard to believe that they each have within them an inner poet. Here, then, are a few suggestions to help you compose your poems. I share my own poems not because I think they are especially good but merely to share my own creative process in hopes that it might encourage you.

A. *Play with a particular sound.*

In *Writing the Natural Way* (1983, 122), Gabrielle Rico discusses the use of sounds as a basis for beginning a poem. Thus one way we can write a poem is by playing with sounds. Here's how it worked for me:

1. Pick the sound you like.
> M. Mmmmmmmmmm.

2. Pick a word that begins with that sound and that also sounds good to you.
> Mud.

3. Try making a phrase using the word and sound.
> My mud
> My mucky mud

4. Now use the words and sound and let it become a poem.
> My mother minds
> My mucky mud—
> But I don't!

B. *Use an image or images from a particularly significant experience.* Rather than describing the event, start with the images that have continued to linger in your mind.

For four summers, I have attended a remarkable week-long camp for children who either have cancer or are in remission. The experience has changed me. When I tried to capture the images of that first year, here is what emerged:

> Young men and women
> cooling their rage with laughter.
> An errant skunk.
> Missing limbs and haunting beauty.
> Loneliness here and there
> in the eyes of campfire watchers.
> Thunder at 3 P.M.
> Sunrises—a glimpse of God's smile
> on little ones wise beyond their years.

A sadness in places as word passes
that someone didn't make it.
Hope—joyful, shouting, prank-filled hope
given as a gift
by young teachers
to one who has so much to learn.

C. *Begin with a particular image that has stayed with you for
reasons unknown.*

Sometimes we glimpse something and the memory of that
image haunts us. We don't know why, for consciously we cannot connect it with anything. My own thought is that the image
has attached itself to a poem inside of us that is trying to come
out. For years I retained in the back of my mind an image from
my job as a postal carrier. As I was delivering mail one day I
saw an old man, who was attached to an oxygen machine, sitting on a porch. The memory of that man haunted me for years
until it resurfaced as this poem:

Black Lung Marriage

An old coal miner
rocks on his front porch
talking to any who will listen
as he points to his oxygen machine.

"How do you like her?
She's a looker, eh?
Makes me breathe real heavy, know
    what I mean?"

He tries to laugh
but coughs so deep
it hurts his ribs
then sucks on his machine.
"Oh, she hisses a lot.
She hates the dust that lines my lungs
and is always after me
to cough it up.
What a nag!"

He sucks some more
then rubs his ribs.

"Sometimes I wish she'd let me die,
　ya know?"

Poems about our past are commonly used in the form of poetry therapy. We may use the language of poetry not so much to capture a memory but to capture its impact on us. The following poem, written with love, describes an impression from my own home when I was growing up:

All Good Irishmen Read the Obituaries

Two old people sit in a dimly-lit
orange glowing room.
He reads his paper.
She sits across the room
reading her romance novel,
her face without expression.

"Oh-oh. Charley Cole died."
"Oh my. When? How?"
"Last night. Heart attack."
"Oh dear."
"Mmm-hmm. Funeral's Wednesday."
"I'll fix a plate to send."
"Mm-hmm."

"Look here. Ed McGinnis passed away."
"Who?"
"Eddie McGinnis."
"Oh."
"Sixty-three. He was sixty-three."
"Mm-hmm."

Slowly, she closes her book and sighs.
She gathers the empty cups
and shuffles to her kitchen.

He carefully folds his paper
having done his duty,
thankful that for one more day
his name was not there.

As contemplatives we may find the language of poetry a more
satisfactory method in which to capture moments of wonder
in our lives. Coming full circle, then, here is my own remem-
brance of that marvelous homer by Bill Mazeroski. Should
you ever have a chance to watch a replay of the seventh
game, don't miss it!

Autumn 1960

Fall.
Burning leaves.
Light jackets.
The Series.

My Braves left long behind.
The vaguely-known Pirates
squeezing the hated Yankees
into a seventh game.

Fall.

Red, yellow, orange leaves
littered everywhere.
Scraped into piles for jumping.
But not today.
Pirates behind.

An errant ball, a misplaced pebble.
(Forgive me, Tony.
I cheered as you clutched
your damaged throat.)

Walking home
Radio pressed to a not-yet chilled ear.
Hal Smith (do I have his card?)
Now I run, in time for the 8th and 9th.

> Long shadows.
> Chipmunks scurry.
> Two outs. It's Maz's hour.
> He swings
> and Yogi watches,
> like a little boy
> who let go of his balloon.
>
> Nighttime.
> Do I hear geese?
> Do they know
> what happened today?[1]

Please try, won't you? Write a poem, then read it aloud to a loved one. (The act of reading one's poems out loud seems to enhance the emotional sense of the poem.) Your poems may not only be the action of your contemplation, they may be the messages you bring back to others.

Teachers for Contemplatives

Thankfully we have available to us many experts on the topic of wonder. They are somewhat unexpected teachers, however, in that they are usually short and operate, at times, from a somewhat limited language base. Nevertheless they are truly masters. Of course the teachers I am talking about are our children and our grandchildren.

For a child, a sprouting plant is a true wonder. A chance encounter with a deer is a treasured memory. Even a meeting with a person in a wheelchair is cause for intense observation. You may be thinking, but children have such short attention spans. Not when the object to behold is wondrous!

There is no better instruction in contemplative wonder than to plant a garden with a child. The child's eagerness and impatience is followed by intense excitement at the first shoots. Then more impatience and eagerness until the first fruits begin to appear. This excitement is in turn followed by—more impatience and eagerness. Finally the moment of harvest arrives. I will long remember my son Andrew proudly displaying the watermelon that he grew. After his picture was taken, he stood smiling and, looking at his mother, said simply, "Mom, I'm happy." What a wonderful lesson for those of us who lose our sense of wonder amidst the hurrying and bustle of everyday life.

Another way to instill a sense of wonder in a child is to take him or her on a camping trip. To the child, a day and night in the forest is a journey filled with awe. The child's anticipation of seeing the first star or the growing fascination with the flickering lights of the campfire and the blackening hot dog can be quite instructive. So, too, is the child's tentative inquiries about sounds in the night. Older folks can learn a lot from children. Ponder for a moment the marvelous nature of the world—its hammers and harmonicas, its kittens and cows, and especially its newborn babies. Show them to a child and pay careful attention to the lessons that they bring.

Trailheads for Mystics

Mystical moments cannot be sought or created. They find us. All that we can offer is the openness and faith that these moments are possible.

Using this awareness to strengthen faith and enhance openness, we can, however, identify mystical moments that we have experienced in the past. Think in terms of feeling connected. Most of us can identify moments of deep connectedness with those we love.

Sexual union is a powerful source of mystical experience but only when it is approached with openness, trust, and vulnerability. From such a framework and with a goal only to give and receive pleasure, a couple can enjoy deep connectedness, which is, by definition a mystical experience. Frequently long-term couples experience a connectedness that offers a glimmer into the realm of the mystic, such as when they anticipate one another's thoughts.

Connectedness may also occur between parent and child. Fortunately I have felt deep moments of kinship with each of my children. These moments of shared joy, which tend to involve nature, music, or poetry, are treasured memories.

A powerful and accessible sense of connectedness comes to those who are able to manifest the image of the wounded healer. A concept found in many cultures, it reflects the wisdom that our wounds can be a vital source of compassion and a sense of commonality. The image of the wounded healer forms the heart of the Twelve-Step program and one that has been adopted by a growing number in the healing professions. A note of caution is necessary, however.

Few words are used more inappropriately than the phrase "I know how you feel." I don't know how anyone else feels unless they tell me, and even then I may still miss the mark. Further I can only share a comparable experience and hope that it approximates another person's in a similar way. In other words, if I tap into my own woundedness as a basis for a possible connection with you, I must still be respectful and assume that my experience is not the same as yours. It is up to you to determine whether or not I know how you feel. Therapists and other professional as well as nonprofessional helpers, even if they view themselves as wounded healers, would do well to drop the well-worn phrase altogether. A better alternative may be "This is what I experienced. Perhaps my sharing of that might help in some way?"

A Valued Teacher to the Mystic

Great thinkers through the ages from Henry David Thoreau to William James to Loren Eiseley have commented on the mystical aspect of nature. But how often do we truly connect with nature? How often are we genuinely aware that we humans and the rest of God's creation are, in fact, intertwined? More often than not, we go to the woods, the beach, the desert, or the mountains to escape from our day-to-day existence. How many of you have been at campgrounds only to hear loud music drown out the songbird? How many of you have heard the sound of beer cans being opened long into the night?

As William James and others have noted, mystical experiences have a spontaneous quality about them. Thus we cannot go to the woods "to have a mystical experience." The harder we pursue it, the more elusive it becomes. But we can go to the woods with our senses open. For example, I can go with the specific purpose to contemplate. From this contemplation may come a moment of mystical connection. Perhaps I may unexpectedly encounter another person or a wild animal. These encounters can evoke the appearance of the mystic.

A starting point for openness is to recall sensory experiences from encounters with nature. Here is my own list:

Sight—an unexpected vision of a golden eagle;
Sound—walking along a trail in the dark and hearing
    the sound of a deer ambling through a nearby stream;
Touch—the feel of damp sand oozing between my toes
    as a wave washes over and under my feet;
Taste—ice-cold, clear stream water;
Smell—the scent of wild sage

I find if I enter the forest with my senses alert, I am more open to the possibility of connection.

Not everyone, however, has access to the woods, the desert, or the ocean. How, then, can we grow as mystics in the middle of concrete? Thankfully the sun rises and sets everywhere. Nature also puts on displays of power and majesty with rain and snowstorms. Here in the Southwest, for example, we have the wonderful mystery of the desert. These natural occurrences can all be doorways to the mystical.

For some, however, skyscapers or tenements block out the rays of the sun. Others can't afford the price of admission to national parks, much less the cost of transportation to get there. My enjoyment of the outdoors, then, may give way to a growing awareness that the evil of poverty deprives others of the spiritual experiences of nature. My resulting emotions of sadness and anger may start my movement toward the phase of the prophet.

Trailheads for Prophets

In chapter 6, we touched on the issue of discernment. How might the prophet know where to direct action? A starting point is to identify those current issues that stir one's passion. What types of headlines evoke anger? sadness? What documentaries or news reports have moved you? Try to think of what agitates you, not what *should* be a concern.

Think, too, of those issues that you try to avoid. If you change the channel when a news story comes on about the homeless, what are you avoiding? Does this not suggest a blind spot?

The prophet derives personal growth from "interference." The activity of the prophet may, in fact, only be successful when the prophet has grown, has learned something new about himself or herself. Such new information may move the prophet back into the movement of the meditator.

Some issues involve the matter of being "different." For personal growth, we must try to reach out to those whom we judge to be different.

From a personal perspective, I would like to mention three issues of importance to me:

1. *The environment.* I find myself outraged and saddened by oil spills or forest fires. Watching televised images of dying birds, their feathers coated with oil, is the visual definition of sin.
2. *Economics.* I have tried to avoid issues relating to economics, fearing that I will not be able to grasp their sometimes complex principles. I am only now beginning to recognize the importance of economics on society and so I am trying to educate myself.
3. *Distribution of wealth.* As noted earlier, I tend to distrust people of wealth. But I have also begun to realize that, to function as a prophet, it is misguided for me to harbor resentment. I would do better to actively pursue simplicity in my own life and, through writing, encourage others to do so.

Awareness of one's gifts can encourage us to become involved in issues that we care about. Gifts can also allow us to feel a healthy sense of power. If I feel I have done something well, I may detect a sense of both gift and power at work. Fortunately this gift-centered power tends to be beneficial. The challenge here is to recognize that the gift may be transitory or may need to be transformed in order to flourish. Sad are those who lose their gifted power—because of the aging process, for example, or some other form of change—yet cannot accept the loss or cannot allow the gift to transform itself.

Teachers for Prophets

We do not all have access to great prophets such as Mother Teresa. Prophets dream of a better world for themselves, for those they love, and for all of society. Unfortunately many of us have lost the capacity to dream. Others have had to grieve over the loss of a dream because of a change in circumstances or perhaps simply because of age. Some refer to specific types of dreams as visions. For me, a vision is a dream with a general plan of action. In order to have a vision, first we have to recapture the *capacity* for dreaming.

Whether we realize it or not most of us have access to a population of dreamers—teenagers. Teenagers are great dreamers. Ask them what they want to do in life and, invariably, many talk about starting a rock band. But the energy and enthusiasm they put into their dreams is where lessons can be found.

Teenagers are persons who look to the future with a private hope in order to visualize what their lives may be like. Of course, not all teenagers have this luxury. Some, for various reasons—be it drugs, poverty, or crime—have given up the dream entirely. It is our duty as adults to restore a sense of hope and well-being to their shattered lives. Without exception, if I ask these teenagers "What are your dreams for the future?," the response is "I don't know." If I then ask, "Have you given up hope?" the answer is "I guess so." This always saddens me.

When I was between the ages of thirteen and eighteen, I had three dreams: (1) to become a priest; (2) to become a professional baseball player; and (3) to become a famous actor. I have accomplished none of these things. But pieces of each of these dreams have stayed with me and, I like to think, have been transformed. I am not a priest, but I do hold onto the hope of a close relationship with God. I am not a professional baseball player, but I have not lost the love of the game and, through baseball, have found a poet inside of me. I am not a famous actor, but I have found much joy and a creative outlet on stages in Scranton, Pennsylvania, and El Paso, Texas.

At this point, you may wish to list the dreams from your own adolescence. Have you achieved them? If not, have they become transformed? If they were lost along the way, what blocked their realization? Perhaps, like me, you lacked the necessary skills and self-discipline. Perhaps you were defeated by self-doubt. Or, perhaps, others stood in your way. You may want to assess the current status of those dreams. Do they still gnaw at you or have they become deferred, in danger of drying up, "like a raisin in the sun," in the words of Langston Hughes (1974, 268)?

Not all of our dreams are of great significance. Several years ago, after seeing the film *Field of Dreams* countless times, I asked myself what my dreams were now. I had two: to see a baseball game at Fenway Park (which I did!) and to have a book published. *Becoming a Modern Contemplative* constitutes my third book.

Prophets also need teachers. For me, the most courageous teachers have been children suffering from cancer. Are children with cancer saints? Absolutely not. I have met some children who, at times, are downright aggravating! But, in their own way, they all are teachers of courage. Each child I have met has refused to be bitter. Each has fought back. Unfortunately, despite all the efforts, some do die, but not without first offering us the true lesson of existence—we must continue to move *into* life, not away from it. The lessons they can teach are small ones, such as the memory of one young woman who had lost her foot to cancer yet insisted on participating in the camp's equestrian program. A young man (the same one mentioned in chapter 1 who played the Garth Brooks song) hesitated to mount the horse. "You know," I said to him, "you've faced things more scary than that horse." He paused. "You're right," he said. The look of satisfaction on his face when he sat atop the horse stands as a lesson in courage for any modern contemplative. One year later, both young people returned to camp. The young woman, with the aid of her prothesis, proudly mounted a horse, riding like a professional. The young man pursued riding lessons and became an accomplished equestrian.

Everywhere can be found people trying to face, with courage, some insurmountable challenge. They may be at your local hospice or through your local AIDS support network, at various emergency shelters, on pediatric wards. Some may have given in to fear or resentment and turned bitter. But many have not. You may find it very instructive to spend time listening to these teachers.

Trailheads for Clowns

While working on this book, I found myself searching for an image that would somehow integrate the four primary images. By chance I learned that a priest friend had a secret. He would occasionally entertain at children's parties by dressing up as a clown. I was further reminded that some churches sponsor a clown ministry. Finally, as I discussed this image with a friend, he reminded me that Saint Francis of Assisi was called not only God's Fool but also God's Clown. I had my image! I needed, however, to learn more about clowns and so turned to Mark Stolzenberg's book *Be a Clown!* (1989), which is part hands-on instruction manual and part exercises (the latter are both fun and enlightening). One exercise asks us to nonverbally mime contrasting attitudes such as "sophisticated-obscene," "proud-humble," and "serious-humor." Using these exercises, I discovered how out-of-touch I am with my body, how restricted I have become in movement (clowns, remember, must play their movements broadly). Such constraints may be a problem. After all, how effective as a prophet can I be if my energy is so inhibited and contained?

Stolzenberg also spends much time inviting potential clowns to attend to the image they wish to portray. He discusses three common types of clowns:

1. *The white-faced clown* is both sophisticated and aristocratic, serious and proper. Typically the white-faced clown represents authority. (It may be that this type of clown accounts for the main reason that some people do not like clowns or even fear them. The fear seems to have something to do with the real face being hidden underneath the greasepaint).

2. *The auguste* or *noble clown* may appear stupid and often is disruptive, especially the white-faced clown. The auguste clown projects simplicity, even naivete.

3. *The character clown* is usually an exaggeration of an everyday type of individual. Examples include Carol Burnett's washerwoman or Jackie Gleason's Poor Soul and Reginald Van Gleason III. Danny Kaye often created memorable characters, such as his famous symphony conductor.

What does this have to do with prophets? For one thing, it may help you focus on how you would like to come across to others. Some persons may come across as white-faced clowns in the sense of presenting themselves as "in the know" or, more dangerously, as always being "right." Similarly we see many white-faced clowns on both sides of the abortion issue. Some pro-life advocates are so doctrinaire that they are quite harsh and judgmental toward women who genuinely ache over a pregnancy or an aborted fetus. By the same token, some pro-choice supporters angrily dismisss members of the right-to-life movement as "kooks" and "clinic bombers." Thus you may want to be aware of how you deliver your message, trying to capture more the simplicity of the auguste clown rather than the arrogance of the white-faced clown.

The training of the clown can also offer insight into our *persona,* that is, our public self. In dream imagery, persona is often represented by clothing and, indeed, clowns pay much attention to costume. Stolzenberg states that to "discover your clown," you need to pay careful attention to makeup, character, motivation, a specific walk and voice, even a theme song—all are intended to convey a particular message or impression.

Suppose then that you were selected to deliver a speech to a political group on a topic of some importance to you. How would you dress? Would you come across as aggressive? Would you try to be funny?

In a similar vein, a helpful technique is to select any issue that means a lot to you and assume the opposite position. Such a stance can, on the one hand, moderate your temptation to always be right. On the other hand, it may make your arguments more convincing since you will now be able to communicate the opposing opinion with a real understanding.

In learning the skills of a clown, then, we may be internalizing the way of the modern contemplative.

Teacher of the Clown's Way

To identify teachers of the clown's way, make a list of persons who best represent qualities found in each of the four phases of the modern contemplative. The following table might help:

Phase	Outstanding Qualities	Example
Meditator	Self-honesty	
Contemplative	Capacity for wonder	
	Minimal need to control	
	Poetic	
Mystic	Compassionate	
Prophet	Idealistic	
	Courageous	

Don't forget also to list persons who capture the stances that extend across all phases:

Stance	Example
Simplicity	
Self-discipline	
Detachment	
Sensuality	
Gratitude	

If one particular name tends to appear consistently, consider whether that person has a capacity for self-effacing humor. If so, such an individual may be a very important teacher for you.

Another possibility is to use names of famous people in history. One historic person who captures many of the clown's qualities is Saint Francis of Assisi. It is no accident that he has become known as God's Fool. His self-effacing humor certainly captures the elements of a clown yet he manifests every stance and every phase of the modern contemplative. Even though he no longer graces this earth, his life continues to be a very important influence on me.

Of course, none of these trailheads or teachers constitute an exhaustive list, for that is part of the beauty for those who aspire to the image of the modern contemplative. Throughout our life, God manages to place guides and teachers in our path to prevent us from losing our way.

Conclusion

As I look back over all the work that is required to become a modern contemplative, I find myself, at times, overwhelmed and discouraged. How can I hope to aspire to such an image when so much seems to be involved? My journaling is inconsistent. Solitude sometimes scares me. Companionship is difficult since I don't trust people too easily. One of my most sacred places—Guadalupe National Park—is in ashes. Worse, the stances appear beyond reach. Occasionally I want to accumulate more things. Self-discipline remains a major problem. I am at odds with my body. I often lapse into self-pity. And the phases? They may seem more of a lifestyle than I can handle. I allow other issues to take priority over meditation. Most likely, I will have a problem with control for the rest of my life. I often feel more disconnected than connected. All of which leads me to ask how can I see myself as a prophet?

In the midst of such despair, I feel hope. I don't know where such a path will take me. What I do see is that the phases of the modern contemplative, if sought, will make me a better person, a better lover. My loving of others will always be imperfect but the path of the modern contemplative makes the likelihood of improvement all that more possible, so that perhaps one day my love may even be unconditional. I want very much to be a good lover, and I want to start with those closest to me because it is often with those whom we are closest to that our loving is most flawed. In the midst of my discouragement, I take great comfort in the thoughts of author Norman Maclean. In the film version of his classic novella, *A River Runs through It,* the preacher offers a thoughtful sermon after the senseless death of his youngest son Paul.

Each one of us here today will at one time in our lives, look upon a loved one in need and ask the same question. . . . "We are willing, Lord, but what, if anything is needed?" For it is true that we can seldom help those closest to us. Either we don't know what part of *ourselves* to give, or more often than not, the part we have to give . . . is not wanted. And so it is those we live with and should know who elude us. But we can *still* love them. We can love—completely—without complete understanding . . . (Friedenberg, 186; see also Maclean, 104).

I long to love those close to me completely without needing to fully understand them. The path of the modern contemplative offers the best hope that such love is, in fact, possible. I encourage everyone who is drawn to its path to follow it but, initially at least, to direct your learnings to those who are closest to you.

Let us all try to live simply with those we love. Let us try not to control them. Let us hold one another and laugh together. Let us be consistent in our loving. And let us always be grateful for the loving that we do receive.

Notes

Chapter 1: The Stances

1. According to legend, Saint Francis declared freedom from his father and his father's considerable riches by discarding his clothing in the village square. By doing so, Saint Francis symbolically abandoned his identity as a person of wealth.
2. Twelve Step is the program of recovery developed by Alcoholics Anonymous. See *Alcoholics Anonymous*. 3rd ed. New York: Alcoholics Anonymous World Service, 1976.
3. The Fifth Step of the Twelve-Step program involves sharing one's moral inventory with someone.
4. Alanon, the companion program to AA, provides help and support to spouses of alcoholics.

Chapter 6: The Movement of the Modern Contemplative

1. This driven quality can be explained in rational-emotive terms. Rational-emotive therapy refers to the school of therapy founded by Albert Ellis. Essentially, Ellis claims that our thoughts and expectations give rise to our emotional experiences, particularly unpleasant ones such as guilt and anger. See Albert Ellis and Robert Harper, *A New Guide to Rational Living* (Hollywood, Calif.: Wilshire Books, 1975), for an introduction.
2. Gestalt therapy focuses heavily on catharsis as a curative factor, using methods similar to Carl Jung's technique of active imagination. Fritz Perls is often cited as its founder.
3. The NAMES Project has become better known as the Quilt. The Quilt commemorates the people who have

lost their lives to AIDS. The Quilt's evolution is portrayed in a very moving documentary entitled *Common Threads: Stories from the Quilt.* For more information, contact the NAMES Project Foundation, 2362 Market Street, San Francisco, Calif. 94114.

4. Dr. Martin Luther King, Jr., the leading civil rights figure of the 1960s, was assassinated in Memphis in April 1968; Caesar Chavez was for many years the premier advocate for the rights of agricultural migrant workers; as bishop of San Salvador, Oscar Romero spoke out against government persecution of citizens. He was assassinated in 1980; Mother Teresa has worked tirelessly to serve the needs of India's poor and infirm; Bill W. was cofounder of Alcoholics Anonymous; Larry Kramer is a playwright whose plays have heightened AIDS awareness; Dorothy Day was founder of the Catholic Worker movement in the United States.

Chapter 7: Messengers and Trailheads

1. In the seventh game of the 1960 World Series between the New York Yankees and the Pittsburgh Pirates, events took a fateful turn in the seventh inning. With one runner on first and Pittsburgh behind eight to six, Roberto Clemente hit a ground ball to Yankee shortstop Tony Kubek—a double play would have ended the inning. The ball, however, took a bad bounce, hitting Kubek in the throat and knocking him out of the game. With two runners on base, back-up catcher Hal Smith then hit a three-run home run. The Yankees, however, came back in the eighth inning to tie the game, setting the stage for the Pirates second baseman Bill Mazeroski.

Annotated Bibliography

The following works are intended to serve as additional reference points for the exploration of various topics mentioned in the text.

Techniques of Meditation

A wide variety of approaches to meditation exist. The following works are all fairly straightforward and accessible.

Lawrence LeShan, *How to Meditate* (New York: Bantam, 1975).
A very readable guide that offers an overview of the major schools of meditation, including specific meditative exercises.

Anthony de Mello, *Sadhana: A Way to God* (New York: Doubleday, 1984).
Christian-based guide to meditation influenced by the Desert Fathers. de Mello, however, transcends the Jesus Prayer by incorporating the use of imagery.

Theory and Technique of Dreamwork

First of all, let me discourage the use of popular "dictionaries" found in the New Age section of many bookstores. A more useful approach is to develop a method of decoding dreams. If you think of dreams as a foreign language, linguistic rules would apply.

John Sanford, *Dreams and Healing* (New York: Paulist, 1979).
An excellent introduction to the area of dreamwork and an accessible examination of the theories of Carl Jung.

Jeremy Taylor, *Dreamwork: Techniques for Discovering the Creative Power of Dreams* (New York: Paulist, 1983).
Also Jungian based, this work has several very pragmatic suggestions for discerning meaning in dreams.

Louis M. Savary, Patricia H. Berne, and Stephon K. Williams, *Dreams and Spiritual Growth* (New York: Paulist, 1984).
A highly recommended work that constitutes a veritable smorgasbord of dreamwork techniques. Read it, experiment with the different techniques suggested, then choose what suits you best.

Dictionaries of symbols define the meaning of symbols found across cultures. They can be very helpful, especially when addressing archetypal material. Two that I highly recommend are

Tom Chetwynd, *A Dictionary of Symbols* (London: Paladin Books, 1982).
J. E. Cirlot, *A Dictionary of Symbols* (London: Thames and Hudson, 1978).

Journaling

One approach to learning about journaling is to read the published fruits of writers' journal work. Here are a few of my personal favorites:

William Least Heat Moon, *Blue Highways* (New York: Ballantine, 1982).
Least Heat Moon's journal of his year-long odyssey through the backroads of America is a stirring portrayal of a man in search of his soul.

Henri Nouwen, *The Road to Daybreak: A Spiritual Journey* (New York: Doubleday, 1988).
Nouwen's journal traces his journey through the phases of a modern contemplative as we follow his calling to work with the *anawim* at a L'Arche center in Canada.

These centers welcome physically and emotionally impaired persons who have nowhere else to turn.

Finally, we can learn much about journal work through various meditation pieces, that is, works that do not so much narrate a journey as reflect a central image or theme. Suggested works along this line include:

Paul Brand, and Phillip Yancey, *Fearfully and Wonderfully Made* (Grand Rapids, Mich.: Zondervan Publishing House, 1980).
Dr. Brand is an undiscovered treasure and, in his own right, a modern contemplative. He spent many years working as a physician in India and ultimately came into a great deal of contact with leprosy. *Fearfully and Wonderfully Made* consists of meditations on spirituality based on the workings of our bodies.

L. A. Gainer, *The Hidden Garden* (Huntington, Ind.: Our Sunday Visitor, 1985).
This little book explores spirituality through the metaphor of the author's garden.

Why Time Begins on Opening Day (1984) and *How Life Imitates the World Series* (1982), by Thomas Boswell and published by Penguin, are meditation pieces on baseball. Need I say more?

Modern Contemplatives

We can learn a great deal about the journey of the modern contemplative by studying the lives of some of our greatest examples. Here are some possibilities:

Thomas Merton

The life of this Trappist monk is one of the best examples of someone who followed the path of the modern contemplative. Of value in studying Merton's life are his own famous autobiography, *The Seven-Story Mountain* (New York: Harcourt, Brace, and Co., 1948) and Henri Nouwen's summary of Merton's work, *Thomas Merton: Contemplative Critic* (New York: Harper and Row, 1981).

Black Elk
As presented in John G. Neihardt's *Black Elk Speaks* (New York: Washington Square, 1959), Black Elk's vision quest and prophecies are also a clear portrayal of the journey of the modern contemplative.

Clowns
Saint Francis of Assisi is clearly one of God's most loving clowns. G. K. Chesterton's book *St. Francis of Assisi* (New York: Image Books, 1957) is considered a classic. Personally, I found Murray Bodo's *Tales of St. Francis* (New York: Doubleday, 1988) an enjoyable introduction. It consists of brief stories that, while not necessarily historical, do convey the spirit of Franciscan spirituality.

Morris West, *Clowns of God* (New York: William Morrow and Co., 1981).
Although fictional, this novel gives the concept of the clown an interesting twist. The fictional Pope Gregory XVII decides to publish letters under the pen name of Jeannot le Bouffon (Johnny the Clown). His writings are both childlike and profound—what one might expect from a true clown.

For the works of other great contemplatives, including Abraham Heschel, John Muir, and Bill W., see References Cited.

References Cited

Ackerman, Diane. 1991. *A Natural History of the Senses.* New York: Vintage.

Alcoholics Anonymous. 1976. 3rd ed. New York: Alcoholics Anonymous World Service.

Amiotte, Arthur. 1989. "The Road to the Center." In *I Become Part of It: Sacred Dimensions in Native American Life,* edited by D. M. Dooley and P. Smith. New York: Parabola.

Anthony, Susan B. 1987. *Sidewalk Contemplatives: A Spirituality for Socially Concerned Christians.* New York: Crossroad.

Benson, Herbert. 1976. *The Relaxation Response.* New York: Avon.

Berman, Phillip. 1990. *The Search for Meaning: Americans Talk about What They Believe and Why.* New York: Ballantine.

Bernanos, Georges. 1954. *The Diary of a Country Priest.* New York: Image.

Berry, Thomas. 1988. *The Dream of the Earth.* San Francisco: Sierra Club.

Booth, Leo. 1991. *When God Becomes a Drug.* Los Angeles: Jeremy P. Tarcher.

Boswell, Thomas. 1990. *The Heart of the Order.* New York: Penguin.

Bradley, Ian. 1990. *God Is Green: Ecology for Christians.* New York: Image.

Bradshaw, John. 1988. *Healing the Shame that Binds You.* Deerfield, Fla.: Health Communications.

Brewi, Janice, and Anne Brennan. 1990. *Celebrate Midlife: Jungian Archetypes and Midlife Spirituality.* New York: Crossroad.

Clift, Jean, and Wallace Clift. 1988. *The Hero Journey in Dreams.* New York: Crossroad.

Dillard, Annie. 1984. *Holy the Firm*. New York: Harper and Row.

——. 1985. *Pilgrim at Tinker Creek*. New York: Perennial Library.

Dollard, Jerry. 1983. *Toward Spirituality: The Inner Journey*. Center City, Minn.: Hazelden.

Dresner, S. H., ed. 1990. *I Asked for Wonder: A Spiritual Anthology of Abraham Joshua Heschel*. New York: Crossroad, 1990.

Foster, Richard J. 1981. *Freedom of Simplicity*. New York: Harper and Row.

Fox, Matthew. 1983. *Original Blessing*. Santa Fe, N. M.: Bear and Co.

——. 1991. *Creation Spirituality: Liberating Gifts for the Peoples of the Earth*. San Francisco: Harper.

Friedenberg, Richard. 1992. *A River Runs through It: Bringing a Classic to the Screen*. With an introduction by Robert Redford. Livingston, Mont.: Clark City Press.

Fromm, Eric. 1956. *The Art of Loving*. New York: Harper and Row.

Frost, Robert. 1979. *The Poetry of Robert Frost*. Edited by E. C. Lathem. New York: Holt, Rinehart, and Winston.

Halberstam, David. 1986. *The Amateurs*. New York: Penguin.

Heschel, Abraham J. 1951. *Man Is Not Alone: A Philosophy of Religion*. New York: Noonday Press.

Hughes, Langston. 1974. "A Dream Deferred." In *Selected Poems of Langston Hughes*. New York: Vintage.

Johnson, Robert. 1983. *We: The Psychology of Romantic Love*. New York: Harper and Row.

Jung, Carl G. 1933. "The Stages of Life." In *Modern Man in Search of a Soul*. New York: Harcourt Brace Jovanovich.

Kazimiroff, Theodore L. 1982. *The Last Algonquian*. New York: Laurel.

Kelsey, Morton. 1980. *Adventure Inward: Christian Growth through Personal Journal Writing*. Minneapolis, Minn.: Augsburg Publishing House.

————. 1986. *Christianity as Psychology*. Minneapolis, Minn.: Augsburg Publishing House.

Kushner, Lawrence. 1990. *Honey from the Rock*. Woodstock, Vt.: Jewish Lights.

————.1992. *God Was in This Place and I, i Did Not Know It*. Woodstock, Vt.: Jewish Lights.

Leaf, Munro. 1946. *The Story of Ferdinand the Bull*. New York: Viking.

Lee, Harper. 1960. *To Kill a Mockingbird*. Philadelphia: J. B. Lippincott.

Lewis, C. S. 1987. *The Lion, the Witch, and the Wardrobe*, adapted by Glyn Robbins. New York: Samuel French.

Linn, Matthew, Sheila Fabricant, and Dennis Linn. 1986. *Healing the Eight Stages of Life*. New York: Paulist.

Maclean, Norman. 1992. *A River Runs through It and Other Stories*. New York: Simon and Shuster.

May, Rollo. 1991. *The Cry for Myth*. New York: W. W. Norton.

Merton, Thomas. 1961. *New Seeds of Contemplation*. New York: New Directions.

————. 1968. *Conjectures of a Guilty Bystander*. Garden City, N. Y.: Image.

Muir, John. 1954. *The Wilderness World of John Muir*. Boston: Houghton-Mifflin.

Nouwen, Henri. 1979. *The Wounded Healer*. New York: Image.

Patterson, Richard B. 1992. *Encounters with Angels: Psyche and Spirit in the Counseling Situation*. Chicago: Loyola University Press.

————. 1990. *In Search of the Wounded Healer*. Denville, N. J.: Dimension.

Pearson, Carol. 1991. *Awakening the Heroes Within*. San Francisco: Harper.

Progoff, Ira. 1975. *At a Journal Workshop*. New York: Dialogue House.

Raymo, Chet. 1987. *Honey from Stone: A Naturalist's Search for God*. New York: Dodd, Mead, and Co.

Rico, Gabrielle L. 1983. *Writing the Natural Way.* Los Angeles: J. P. Tarcher.

Rohr, Richard. 1992. *Simplicity: The Art of Living.* New York: Crossroad.

Safire, William. 1992. *The First Dissident: The Book of Job in Today's Politics.* New York: Random House.

Segal, Bernard. 1986. *Love, Medicine, and Miracles.* New York: Harper and Row.

Simonton, O. Carl, Stephanie Matthews-Simonton, and James L. Creighton. 1980. *Getting Well Again.* New York: Bantam.

Smith, Huston. 1991. *The World's Religions.* San Francisco: Harper Collins.

Spong, John Shelby. 1992. *Rescuing the Bible from Fundamentalism: A Bishop Rethinks the Meaning of Scripture.* San Francisco: Harper.

Steindl-Rast, David. 1984. *Gratefulness: The Heart of Prayer.* New York: Paulist.

Stolzenberg, Mark. 1989. *Be a Clown!* New York: Sterling.

Thomas, Dylan. 1957. *The Collected Poems of Dylan Thomas.* New York: New Directions.

Tournier, Paul. 1968. *A Place for You.* New York: Harper and Row.

Ulanov, Ann, and Barry Ulanov. 1987. *The Witch and the Clown: Two Archetypes of Human Sexuality.* Wilmette, Ill.: Chiron.

Underhill, Evelyn. 1970. *Mysticism.* New York: Penguin.

W., Bill. 1988. *The Language of the Heart: Bill W.'s Grapevine Writings.* New York: AA Grapevine.

Watzlawick, P., J. Beavin, and D. Jackson. 1967. *Pragmatics of Human Communication.* New York: W. W. Norton.

Wilder, Thornton. 1938. *Our Town.* New York: Harper and Row.

Wolff, Pierre. 1979. *May I Hate God?* New York: Paulist.

Wolpe, David J. 1990. *The Healer of Shattered Hearts: A Jewish View of God.* New York: Penguin.

Index